Prayers That
Avail Much
Volume II

James 5:16

Prayers That Avail Much

Volume II

James 5:16

by
Word Ministries, Inc.

And this is the confidence that we have in him,
that, if we ask any thing according to his will, he
heareth us: and if we know that he hear us,
whatsoever we ask, we know that we have the
petitions that we desired of him.

1 John 5:14,15

Harrison House
Tulsa, Oklahoma

9th Printing
Over 233,000 in Print

Prayers That Avail Much — Volume II
ISBN 0-89274-865-6
Revised Edition
(Formerly ISBN 0-89274-591-6)
Copyright © 1989, 1991 by Word Ministries, Inc.
38 Sloan St.
Roswell, GA 30075

Published by Harrison House, Inc.
P. O. Box 35035
Tulsa, Oklahoma 74153

CONTENTS

II. Intercessory Prayers for Others

Prayers for God's People and Ministries

Prayers for the Needs of Others

Prayers That Avail Much
Volume II

James 5:16

FOREWORD

The prayers in this book are to be used by you for yourself and for others. They are a matter of the heart. Deliberately feed them into your spirit. Allow the Holy Spirit to make the Word a reality in your heart. Your spirit will become quickened to God's Word, and you will begin to think like God thinks and talk like He talks. You will find yourself poring over His Word — hungering for more and more. The Father rewards those who diligently seek Him. (Heb. 11:6.)

Meditate upon the Scriptures listed with these prayers. These are by no means the only Scriptures on certain subjects, but they are a beginning.

These prayers are to be a help and a guide to you in order for you to get better acquainted with your heavenly Father and His Word. Not only does His Word affect your life, but also it will affect others through you, for you will be able to counsel accurately those who come to you for advice. If you cannot counsel someone with the Word, you do not have anything with which to counsel. Walk in God's counsel, and prize His wisdom. (Ps. 1; Prov. 4:7,8.) People are looking for something on which they can depend. When someone in need comes to you, you can point him to that portion in God's Word that is the answer to his problem. You become victorious, trustworthy, and the one with the answer, for your heart is fixed and established on His Word. (Ps. 112.)

Once you begin delving into God's Word, you must commit to ordering your conversation aright. (Ps. 50:23.) That is being a doer of the Word. Faith always has a good report. You cannot pray effectively for yourself, for someone else, or about something and then talk negatively about the matter. (Matt. 12:34-37.) This is being double-minded, and a double-minded man receives *nothing* from God. (James 1:6-8.)

In Ephesians 4:29,30 AMP it is written:

> Let no foul or polluting language, nor evil word, nor unwholesome or worthless talk [ever] come out of your mouth; but only such [speech] as is good and beneficial to the spiritual progress of others, as is fitting to the need and the occasion, that it may be a blessing and give grace (God's favor) to those who hear it.
>
> And do not grieve the Holy Spirit of God, (do not offend, or vex, or sadden Him) by whom you were sealed (marked, branded as God's own, secured) for the day of redemption — of final deliverance through Christ from evil and the consequences of sin.

Allow these words to sink into your innermost being. Our Father has much, so very much, to say about that little member, the tongue. (James 3.) Give the devil no opportunity by getting into worry, unforgiveness, strife, and criticism. Put a stop to idle and foolish talking. (Eph. 4:27; 5:4.) You are to be a blessing to others. (Gal. 6:10.)

Talk the answer, not the problem. The answer is in God's Word. You must have knowledge of that Word — revelation knowledge. (1 Cor. 2:7-16.)

As an intercessor, unite with others in prayer. United prayer is a mighty weapon that the Body of Christ is to use.

Believe you receive when you pray. Confess the Word. Hold fast to your confession of faith in God's Word. Allow your spirit to pray by the Holy Spirit. Praise God for the victory *now* before any manifestation. *Walk by faith and not by sight.* (2 Cor. 5:7.)

Don't be moved by adverse circumstances. As Satan attempts to challenge you, resist him steadfast in the faith — letting patience have her perfect work. (James 1:4.) Take the Sword of the Spirit and the shield of faith and quench his every fiery dart. (Eph. 6:16,17.) The entire substitutionary work of Christ was for you. Satan is now a defeated foe because Jesus conquered him. (Col. 2:14,15.) Satan is overcome by the blood of the Lamb and the Word of our testimony. (Rev. 12:11.) Fight the good fight of faith. (1 Tim. 6:12.) Withstand the adversary and be firm in faith against his onset — rooted, established, strong, and determined. (1 Pet. 5:9.) Speak God's Word boldly and courageously.

Your desire should be to please and to bless the Father. As you pray in line with His Word, He joyfully hears that you — His child — are living and walking in the Truth. (3 John 4.)

How exciting to know that the prayers of the saints are forever in the throne room. (Rev. 5:8.) Hallelujah!

Praise God for His Word and the limitlessness of prayer in the name of Jesus. It belongs to every child of God. Therefore, run with patience the race that is set before you, looking unto Jesus the author and finisher of your faith. (Heb. 12:1,2.) God's Word is able to build you up and give you your rightful inheritance among all God's set apart ones. (Acts 20:32.)

Commit yourself to pray and to pray correctly by approaching the throne with your mouth filled with His Word!

INTRODUCTION

...The earnest (heart-felt, continued) prayer of
a righteous man makes tremendous power available
— dynamic in its working.

James 5:16 AMP

Prayer is fellowshiping with the Father — a vital,
personal contact with God Who is more than enough.
We are to be in constant communion with Him:

For the eyes of the Lord are upon the righteous
— those who are upright and in right standing with
God — and His ears are attentive (open) to their
prayer....

1 Peter 3:12 AMP

Prayer is not to be a religious form with no power.
It is to be effective and accurate and bring *results.* God
watches over His Word to perform it. (Jer. 1:12.)

Prayer that brings results must be based on God's
Word.

For the Word that God speaks is alive and full
of power — making it active, operative, energizing
and effective; it is sharper than any two-edged sword,
penetrating to the dividing line of the breath of life
(soul) and [the immortal] spirit, and of joints and
marrow [that is, of the deepest parts of our nature]
exposing and sifting and analyzing and judging the
very thoughts and purposes of the heart.

Hebrews 4:12 AMP

13

Prayer is this "living" Word in our mouths. Our mouths must speak forth faith, for faith is what pleases God. (Heb. 11:6.) We hold His Word up to Him in prayer, and our Father sees Himself in His Word.

God's Word is our contact with Him. We put Him in remembrance of His Word (Is. 43:26) placing a demand on His ability in the name of our Lord Jesus. We remind Him that He supplies all of our needs according to His riches in glory by Christ Jesus. (Phil. 4:19.) That Word does not return to Him void — without producing any effect, useless — but it *shall* accomplish that which He pleases and purposes, and it shall prosper in the thing for which He sent it. (Is. 55:11.) Hallelujah!

God did *not* leave us without His thoughts and His ways for we have His Word — His bond. God instructs us to call Him, and He will answer and show us great and mighty things. (Jer. 33:3.) Prayer is to be exciting — not drudgery.

It takes someone to pray. God moves as we pray in faith — believing. He says that His eyes run to and fro throughout the whole earth to show Himself strong in behalf of those whose hearts are blameless toward Him. (2 Chron. 16:9.) We are blameless. (Eph. 1:4.) We are His very own children. (Eph. 1:5.) We are His righteousness in Christ Jesus. (2 Cor. 5:21.) He tells us to come boldly to the throne of grace and *obtain* mercy and find grace to help in time of need — appropriate and well-timed help. (Heb. 4:16.) Praise the Lord!

The prayer armor is for every believer, every member of the Body of Christ, who will put it on and walk in it, for the weapons of our warfare are *not carnal* but mighty through God for the pulling down of the strongholds of the enemy (Satan, the god of this world, and all his demonic forces). Spiritual warfare takes place in prayer. (2 Cor. 10:4, Eph. 6:12,18.)

There are many different kinds of prayer, such as the prayer of thanksgiving and praise, the prayer of dedication and worship, and the prayer that changes *things* (not God). All prayer involves a time of fellowshiping with the Father.

In Ephesians 6, we are instructed to take the Sword of the Spirit which is the Word of God and **pray at all times — on every occasion, in every season — in the Spirit, with all [manner of] prayer and entreaty** (Eph. 6:18 AMP).

In 1 Timothy 2 we are admonished and urged that **petitions, prayers, intercessions and thanksgivings be offered on behalf of all men** (1 Tim. 2:1 AMP). *Prayer is our responsibility.*

Prayer must be the foundation of every Christian endeavor. Any failure is a prayer failure. We are *not* to be ignorant concerning God's Word. God desires for His people to be successful, to be filled with a full, deep, and clear knowledge of His will (His Word), and to bear fruit in every good work. (Col. 1:9-13.) We then bring honor and glory to Him. (John 15:8.) He desires that we know how to pray for **the prayer of the upright is his delight** (Prov. 15:8).

Our Father has not left us helpless. Not only has He given us His Word, but also He has given us the Holy Spirit to help our infirmities when we know not how to pray as we ought. (Rom. 8:26.) Praise God! Our Father has provided His people with every possible avenue to insure their complete and total victory in this life in the name of our Lord Jesus. (1 John 5:3-5.)

We pray to the Father, in the name of Jesus, through the Holy Spirit, according to the Word!

Using God's Word on purpose, specifically, in prayer is one means of prayer, and it is a most effective and accurate means. Jesus said, **The words (truths) that I have been speaking to you are spirit and life** (John 6:63 AMP).

When Jesus faced Satan in the wilderness, He said, ''It is written...it is written...it is written.'' We are to live, be upheld, and sustained by every Word that proceeds from the mouth of God. (Matt. 4:4.)

James, by the Spirit, admonishes that we do not have, because we do not ask. We ask and receive not, because we ask amiss. (James 4:2,3.) We must heed that admonishment now for we are to become experts in prayer rightly dividing the Word of Truth. (2 Tim. 2:15.)

Using the Word in prayer is *not* taking it out of context, for His Word in us is the key to answered prayer — to prayer that brings results. He is able to do exceedingly abundantly above all we ask or think, according to the power that works in us. (Eph. 3:20.) The power lies within God's Word. It is anointed by the Holy Spirit. The Spirit of God does not lead us apart from the Word, for the Word is of the Spirit of God. We apply that Word personally to ourselves and to others — not adding to or taking from it — in the name of Jesus. We apply the Word to the *now* — to those things, circumstances, and situations facing each of us *now*.

Paul was very specific and definite in his praying. The first chapters of Ephesians, Philippians, Colossians, and 2 Thessalonians are examples of how Paul prayed for believers. There are numerous others. *Search them out.* Paul wrote under the inspiration of the Holy Spirit. We can use these Spirit-given prayers today!

In 2 Corinthians 1:11, 2 Corinthians 9:14, and Philippians 1:4, we see examples of how believers prayed one for another — putting others first in their prayer life with *joy.* Our faith does work by love. (Gal. 5:6.) We grow spiritually as we reach out to help others — praying for and with them and holding out to them the Word of Life. (Phil. 2:16.)

Man is a spirit, he has a soul, and he lives in a body. (1 Thess. 5:23.) In order to operate successfully, each of these three parts must be fed properly. The soul or intellect feeds on intellectual food to produce intellectual strength. The body feeds on physical food to produce physical strength. The spirit — the heart or inward man — is the real you, the part that has been reborn in Christ Jesus. It must feed on spirit food which is God's Word in order to produce and develop faith. As we feast upon God's Word, our minds become renewed with His Word, and we have a fresh mental and spiritual attitude. (Eph. 4:23,24.)

Likewise, we are to present our bodies a living sacrifice, holy, acceptable unto God (Rom. 12:1) and not let that body dominate us but bring it into subjection to the spirit man. (1 Cor. 9:27.) God's Word is healing and health to all our flesh. (Prov. 4:22.) Therefore, God's Word affects each part of us — spirit, soul and body. We become vitally united to the Father, to Jesus, and to the Holy Spirit — one with Them. (John 16:13-15, John 17:21, Col. 2:10.)

God's Word, this spirit food, takes root in our hearts, is formed by the tongue, and is spoken out of our mouths. This is creative power. The spoken Word works as we confess it and then apply the action to it.

Be doers of the Word, and not hearers only, deceiving your own selves. (James 1:22.) Faith without works or corresponding action is *dead*. (James 2:17.) Don't be mental assenters — those who agree that the Bible is true but never act on it. *Real faith is acting on God's Word now*. We cannot build faith without practicing the Word. We cannot develop an effective prayer life that is anything but empty words unless God's Word actually has a part in our lives. We are to hold fast to our *confession* of the Word's truthfulness. Our Lord Jesus is the High Priest of our confession (Heb. 3:1), and He is the Guarantee of a better agreement — a more excellent and advantageous covenant. (Heb. 7:22.)

Prayer does not cause faith to work, but faith causes prayer to work. Therefore, any prayer problem is a problem of doubt — doubting the integrity of the Word and the ability of God to stand behind His promises or the statements of fact in the Word.

We can spend fruitless hours in prayer if our hearts are not prepared beforehand. Preparation of the heart, the spirit, comes from meditation in the Father's Word, meditation on what we are in Christ, what He is to us,

18

and what the Holy Spirit can mean to us as we become God-inside minded. As God told Joshua (Josh. 1:8), as we meditate on the Word day and night, and do according to all that is written, then shall we make our way prosperous and have good success. We are to attend to God's Word, submit to His sayings, keep them in the center of our hearts, and put away contrary talk. (Prov. 4:20-24.)

When we use God's Word in prayer, this is *not* something we just rush through uttering once, and we are finished. Do *not* be mistaken. There is nothing "magical" nor "manipulative" about it — no set pattern or device in order to satisfy what we want or think out of our flesh. Instead we are holding God's Word before Him. We confess what He says belongs to us.

We expect His divine intervention while we choose not to look at the things that are seen but at the things that are unseen, for the things that are seen are subject to change. (2 Cor. 4:18.)

Prayer based upon the Word rises above the senses, contacts the Author of the Word and sets His spiritual laws into motion. It is not just saying prayers that gets results, but it is spending time with the Father, learning His wisdom, drawing on His strength, being filled with His quietness, and basking in His love that bring results to our prayers. Praise the Lord!

*   *   *

The prayers in this book are designed to teach and train you in the art of personal confession and intercessory prayer. As you pray them, you will be reinforcing the prayer armor which we have been instructed to put on in Ephesians 6:11. The fabric from which the armor is made is the Word of God. We are to live by every word that proceeds from the mouth of God. We desire the whole counsel of God, because we know it changes us. By receiving that counsel, you will be ... **transformed (changed) by the [entire] renewal of your mind — by its new ideals and attitude — so that you may prove [for yourselves] what is the good and acceptable and perfect will of God, even the thing which is good and acceptable and perfect [in His sight for you]** (Rom. 12:2 AMP).

The prayers of personal confession of the Word of God for yourself can also be used as intercessory prayers for others by simply praying them in the third person, changing the pronouns *I* or *we* to the name of the person or persons for whom you are interceding and adjusting the verbs accordingly.

The prayers of intercession have blanks in which you (individually or as a group) are to fill in the spaces with the name of the person(s) for whom you are praying. These prayers of intercession can likewise be made into prayers of personal confession for yourself (or your group) by inserting your own name(s) and the proper personal pronouns in the appropriate places.

An often-asked question is: "How many times should I pray the same prayer?"

The answer is simple: you pray until you know that the answer is fixed in your heart. After that, you need to repeat the prayer whenever adverse circumstances or long delays cause you to be tempted to doubt that your prayer has been heard and your request granted.

The Word of God is your weapon against the temptation to lose heart and grow weary in your prayer life. When that Word of promise becomes fixed in your heart, you will find yourself praising, giving glory to God for the answer, even when the only evidence you have of that answer is your own faith.

Another question often asked is: "When we repeat prayers more than once, aren't we praying 'vain repetitions'?"

Obviously, such people are referring to the admonition of Jesus when He told His disciples: **And when you pray do not (multiply words, repeating the same ones over and over, and) heap up phrases as the Gentiles do, for they think they will be heard for their much speaking** (Matt. 6:7 AMP). Praying the Word of God is not praying the kind of prayer that the "heathen" pray. You will note in 1 Kings 18:25-29 the manner of prayer that was offered to the gods who could not hear. That is not the way you and I pray. The words that we speak are not vain, but they are spirit and life, and mighty through God to the pulling down of strongholds. We have a God Whose eyes are over the righteous and Whose ears are open to us: when we pray, He hears us.

You are the righteousness of God in Christ Jesus, and your prayers will avail much. They will bring salvation to the sinner, deliverance to the oppressed, healing to the sick, and prosperity to the poor. They will usher in the next move of God in the earth. In addition to affecting outward circumstances and other people, your prayers will also have an effect upon you.

21

In the very process of praying, your life will be changed as you go from faith to faith and from glory to glory.

As a Christian, your first priority is to love the Lord your God with your entire being, and your neighbor as yourself. You are called to be an intercessor, a man or woman of prayer. You are to seek the face of the Lord as you inquire, listen, meditate and consider in the temple of the Lord.

As one of "God's set-apart ones," the will of the Lord for your life is the same as it is for the life of every other true believer: **...seek ye first the kingdom of God, and his righteousness; and all these things shall be added unto you** (Matt. 6:33).

PERSONAL CONFESSIONS

Jesus is Lord over my spirit, my soul, and my body. (Phil. 2:9-11.)

Jesus has been made unto me wisdom, righteousness, sanctification, and redemption. I can do all things through Christ who strengthens me. (1 Cor. 1:30, Phil. 4:13.)

The Lord is my shepherd. I do not want. My God supplies all my need according to His riches in glory in Christ Jesus. (Ps. 23, Phil. 4:19.)

I do not fret or have anxiety about anything. I do not have a care. (Phil. 4:6, 1 Pet. 5:6,7.)

I am the Body of Christ. I am redeemed from the curse, because Jesus bore my sicknesses and carried my diseases in His own body. By His stripes I am healed. I forbid any sickness or disease to operate in my body. Every organ, every tissue of my body functions in the perfection in which God created it to function. I honor God and bring glory to Him in my body. (Gal. 3:13, Matt. 8:17, 1 Pet. 2:24, 1 Cor. 6:20.)

I have the mind of Christ and hold the thoughts, feelings, and purposes of His heart. (1 Cor. 2:16.)

I am a believer and not a doubter. I hold fast to my confession of faith. I decide to walk by faith and practice faith. My faith comes by hearing and hearing by the Word of God. Jesus is the author and the developer of my faith. (Heb. 4:14, Heb. 11:6, Rom. 10:17, Heb. 12:2.)

The love of God has been shed abroad in my heart by the Holy Spirit and His love abides in me richly. I keep myself in the Kingdom of light, in love, in the Word, and the wicked one touches me not. (Rom. 5:5, 1 John 4:16, 1 John 5:18.)

I tread upon serpents and scorpions and over all the power of the enemy. I take my shield of faith and quench his every fiery dart. Greater is He Who is in me than he who is in the world. (Ps. 91:13, Eph. 6:16, 1 John 4:4.)

I am delivered from this present evil world. I am seated with Christ in heavenly places. I reside in the Kingdom of God's dear Son. The law of the Spirit of life in Christ Jesus has made me free from the law of sin and death. (Gal. 1:4, Eph. 2:6, Col. 1:13, Rom. 8:2.)

I fear *not* for God has given me a spirit of power, of love, and of a sound mind. God is on my side. (2 Tim. 1:7, Rom. 8:31.)

I hear the voice of the Good Shepherd. I hear my Father's voice, and the voice of a stranger I will not follow. I roll my works upon the Lord. I commit and trust them wholly to Him. He will cause my thoughts to become agreeable to His will, and so shall my plans be established and succeed. (John 10:27, Prov. 16:3.)

I am a world overcomer because I am born of God. I represent the Father and Jesus well. I am a useful member in the Body of Christ. I am His workmanship recreated in Christ Jesus. My Father God is all the while effectually at work in me both to will and do His good pleasure. (1 John 5:4,5, Eph. 2:10, Phil. 2:13.)

I let the Word dwell in me richly. He who began a good work in me will continue until the day of Christ. (Col. 3:16, Phil. 1:6.)

PART I
PERSONAL PRAYERS

1
TO PRAY

Father, in the name of Jesus, I offer up thanksgiving that You have called me to be a fellow workman — a joint promoter and a laborer together — with and for You. I commit myself to pray and not to turn coward — faint, lose heart, or give up.

Fearlessly and confidently and boldly I draw near to the throne of grace that I may receive mercy and find grace to help in good time for every need — appropriate help and well-timed help, coming just when I (and others) need it. This is the confidence that I have in You, that, if I ask anything according to Your will, You hear me: and if I know that You hear me, whatsoever I ask, I know that I have the petitions that I desired of You.

When I do not know what prayer to offer and how to offer it worthily as I ought, I thank You, Father, that the (Holy) Spirit comes to my aid and bears me up in my weakness (my inability to produce results). He, the Holy Spirit, goes to meet my supplication and pleads in my behalf with unspeakable yearnings and groanings too deep for utterance. And He Who searches the hearts of men knows what is in the mind of the (Holy) Spirit. The Holy Spirit intercedes and

29

pleads in behalf of the saints according to and in harmony with God's will. Therefore, I am assured and know that (God being a partner in my labor) all things work together and are [fitting into a plan] for my good, because I love God and am called according to [His] design and purpose.

I do not fret or have any anxiety about anything, but in every circumstance and in everything by prayer and petition [definite requests] with thanksgiving continue to make my wants (and the wants of others) known to God. Whatever I ask for in prayer, I believe that it is granted to me, and I will receive it.

The earnest (heartfelt, continued) prayer of a righteous man makes tremendous power available — dynamic in its working. Father, I live in You — abide vitally united to You — and Your words remain in me and continue to live in my heart. Therefore I ask whatever I will and it shall be done for me. When I bear (produce) much fruit (through prayer), You, Father, are honored and glorified. Hallelujah!

Scripture References

1 Corinthians 3:9 AMP   Philippians 4:6 AMP
Luke 18:1 AMP   Mark 11:24 AMP
Hebrews 4:16 AMP   James 5:16b AMP
1 John 5:14,15   John 15:7,8 AMP
Romans 8:26-29 AMP

2

TO PUT ON THE ARMOR OF GOD

In the name of Jesus, I put on the whole armor of God, that I may be able to stand against the wiles of the devil, for I wrestle not against flesh and blood, but against principalities, powers, the rulers of the darkness of this world, and against spiritual wickedness in high places.

Therefore, I take unto myself the whole armor of God, that I may be able to withstand in the evil day, and having done all, to stand. I stand, therefore, having my loins girt about with truth. Your Word, Lord, which is truth, contains all the weapons of my warfare which are not carnal, but mighty through God to the pulling down of strongholds.

I have on the breastplate of righteousness; which is faith and love. My feet are shod with the preparation of the Gospel of peace. In Christ Jesus I have peace, and pursue peace with all men. I am a minister of reconciliation proclaiming the good news of the Gospel.

I take the shield of faith, wherewith I am able to quench all the fiery darts of the wicked, the helmet of salvation *(holding the thoughts, feeling, and purpose of God's heart)* and the sword of the Spirit, which is the Word of God. In the face of all trials, tests, temptations and tribulation, I cut to pieces the snare of the enemy by speaking the Word of God. Greater is He that is in me than he that is in the world.

Thank You, Father, for the armor. I will pray at all times — on every occasion, in every season — in the Spirit, with all [manner of] prayer and entreaty. To that end I will keep alert and watch with strong purpose and perseverance, interceding in behalf of all the saints. My power and ability and sufficiency are from God Who has qualified me as a minister and a dispenser of a new covenant [of salvation through Christ]. Amen.

Scripture References

Ephesians 6:11-14a	Psalm 34:14
John 17:17b	2 Corinthians 5:18
2 Corinthians 10:4	Ephesians 6:16,17 AMP
Ephesians 6:14b,15 AMP	1 John 4:4b
Ephesians 2:14	2 Corinthians 3:5,6 AMP

3

TO GLORIFY GOD

In view of [all] the mercies of God, I make a decisive dedication of my body — presenting all my members and faculties — as a living sacrifice, holy (devoted, consecrated) and well pleasing to You, God, which is my reasonable (rational, intelligent) service and spiritual worship. It is [not in my own strength] for it is You, Lord, Who is all the while effectually at work in me — energizing and creating in me the power and desire — both to will and work for Your good pleasure and satisfaction and delight.

Father, I will not draw back or shrink in fear, for then Your soul would have no delight or pleasure in me. I was bought for a price — purchased with a preciousness and paid for, made Your very own. So, then, I honor You, Lord, and bring glory to You in my body.

I called on You in the day of trouble; You delivered me, and I shall honor and glorify you. I rejoice because You delivered me and drew me to Yourself out of the control and dominion of darkness (*obscurity*) and transferred me into the kingdom of the Son of Your love. I will confess and praise You, O Lord my God, with my whole (united) heart; and I will glorify Your name for evermore.

As a bond servant of Jesus Christ, I receive and develop the talents which have been given me, for I would have You say of me, "Well done, you upright (honorable, admirable) and faithful servant!" I make use of the gifts (faculties, talents, qualities) according to the grace given me. I let my light so shine before men that they may see my moral excellence and my praiseworthy, noble and good deeds, and recognize and honor and praise and glorify my Father Who is in heaven.

In the name of Jesus, I allow my life to lovingly express truth in all things — speaking truly, dealing truly, living truly. Whatever I do — no matter what it is — in word or deed, I do everything in the name of the Lord Jesus and in [dependence upon] His Person, giving praise to God the Father through Him. Whatever may be my task, I work at it heartily (from the soul), as [something done] for the Lord and not for men. To God the Father be all glory and honor and praise. Amen.

Scripture References (AMP)

Romans 12:1	Matthew 25:21
Philippians 2:13	Romans 12:6
Hebrews 10:38b	Matthew 5:16
1 Corinthians 6:20	Ephesians 4:15
Psalm 50:15	Colossians 3:17
Colossians 1:13	Colossians 3:23
Psalm 86:12	

4

TO SANCTIFICATION

Father, in the name of Jesus, I commit myself to a sanctified life — a life of holiness, pleasing to You.

Your Word says to wash ourselves and make ourselves clean, to cease to do evil and learn to do well. Therefore, Father, I repent and turn from any sin in my life and wash myself with the water of the Word. I cleanse myself from all filthiness of the flesh and spirit, perfecting holiness in fear and reverence of You, Lord.

Father, I receive Your forgiveness now and thank You for it, because Your Word says You are faithful and just to forgive us our sins and to cleanse us from all unrighteousness. Thank You that Jesus has been made unto me wisdom, righteousness, sanctification, and redemption. Lord Jesus, You sanctify me through Your truth: Your Word is truth.

I submit myself to You, Lord — spirit, soul, and body. I commit to change whatever needs to be changed in my life, because the desire of my heart is to be a vessel unto honor, sanctified, and fitting for the Master's use and prepared for every good work.

Thank You, Lord, that I eat the good of the land, because I am willing and obedient.

Scripture References

Isaiah 1:16,17

Ephesians 5:26

2 Corinthians 7:1

1 John 1:8,9

1 Corinthians 1:30

John 17:17

2 Timothy 2:21

Isaiah 1:19

5

TO BEAR FRUIT

Lord Jesus, You said in John 15:16 that You have chosen us and ordained us that we should go and bring forth fruit and that our fruit should remain, that whatsoever we shall ask of the Father in Your name, He may give it to us.

The Apostle Paul said to be filled with the fruit of righteousness and that he desired that fruit might abound to our account. Therefore, I commit myself to bring forth the fruit of the spirit: love, joy, peace, longsuffering, gentleness, goodness, faith, meekness, and temperance. I renounce and turn from the fruit of the flesh, because I am Christ's and have crucified the flesh with its affections and lusts.

A seed cannot bear fruit unless it first falls into the ground and dies. I confess that I am crucified with Christ: nevertheless I live; yet not I but Christ lives in me. And the life that I now live in the flesh I live by the faith of the Son of God, who loved me and gave Himself for me.

Father, I thank you that I am good ground, that I hear Your Word and understand it, and that the Word bears fruit in my life — sometimes a hundredfold, sometimes sixty, sometimes thirty. I am like a tree planted by the rivers of water that brings forth fruit in its season. My leaf shall not wither, and whatever I do shall prosper.

Father, thank You for filling me with the knowledge of Your will in all wisdom and spiritual understanding, that I may walk worthy of You, Lord, being fruitful in every good work and increasing in the knowledge of You.

Scripture References

John 15:16
Philippians 1:11
Philippians 4:17
Galatians 5:22-24
John 12:24

Galatians 2:20
Matthew 13:23
Psalm 1:3
Colossians 1:9,10

6

TO HELP OTHERS

Father, in the name of Jesus, I will do unto others as I would have them do unto me. I eagerly pursue and seek to acquire [this] *(agape)* love — I make it my aim, my great quest in life.

Father, in the name of Jesus, I will esteem and look upon and be concerned for not [merely] my own interest, but also for the interest of others as they pursue success. I am strong in the Lord, and in the power of His might. I will, on purpose, in the name of Jesus, make it a practice to please (make happy) my neighbor, *(boss, co-worker, teacher, parent, child, brother, etc.)* for his good and for his true welfare, to edify him — that is, to strengthen him and build him up in all ways — spiritually, socially and materially.

Father, in the name of Jesus, I will therefore encourage (admonish, exhort) others and edify — strengthen and build up — others.

Father, in the name of Jesus, I love my enemies *(as well as my business associates, fellow church members, neighbors, those in authority over me)* and am kind and do good — doing favors so that someone derives benefit from them. I lend expecting and hoping for nothing in return, but considering nothing as lost and

39

despairing of no one. Then my recompense (my reward) will be great — rich, strong, intense, and abundant — and I will be a son of the Most High; for He is kind and charitable and good to the ungrateful and selfish and wicked. I am merciful — sympathetic, tender, responsive, and compassionate — even as my Father is [all these]. I am an imitator of God, my Father — therefore, I walk in love.

Thank You, Father, for imprinting Your laws upon my heart, and inscribing them on my mind — on my inmost thoughts and understanding. According to Your Word, as I would like and desire that men would do to me, I do exactly so to them, in the name of Jesus.

Scripture References

Luke 6:31	1 Thessalonians 5:11 AMP
1 Corinthians 14:1 AMP	Luke 6:35,36 AMP
Philippians 2:4 AMP	Ephesians 5:1,2 AMP
Ephesians 6:10	Hebrews 10:16b AMP
Romans 15:2 AMP	Luke 6:31 AMP

7

ADORATION

"Hallowed Be Thy Name"

Our Father, which art in heaven, hallowed be Thy Name.

Bless the Lord, O my soul: and all that is within me, bless Your Holy Name. I adore You and make known to You my adoration and love this day.

I bless Your Name, *Elohim,* the Creator of heaven and earth, Who was in the beginning. It is You Who made me, and You have crowned me with glory and honor. You are the God of might and strength. Hallowed be Thy Name!

I bless Your Name, *El-Shaddai,* the God Almighty of Blessings. You are the Breasty One Who nourishes and supplies. You are All-Bountiful and All-Sufficient. Hallowed be Thy Name!

I bless Your Name, *Adonai,* my Lord and my Master. You are Jehovah — the Completely Self-Existing One, always present, revealed in Jesus Who is the same yesterday, today and forever. Hallowed be Thy Name!

I bless Your Name, *Jehovah-Jireh,* the One Who sees my needs and provides for them. Hallowed be Thy Name!

I bless Your Name, *Jehovah-Rapha,* my Healer and the One Who makes bitter experiences sweet. You sent Your Word and healed me. You forgave all my iniquities and You healed all my diseases. Hallowed be Thy Name!

I bless Your Name, *Jehovah-M'Kaddesh,* the Lord my Sanctifier. You have set me apart for Yourself. Hallowed be Thy Name!

Jehovah-Nissi, You are my Victory, my Banner, and my Standard. Your banner over me is love. When the enemy shall come in like a flood, You will lift up a standard against him. Hallowed be Thy Name!

Jehovah-Shalom, I bless Your Name. You are my Peace — the peace which transcends all understanding, which garrisons and mounts guard over my heart and mind in Christ Jesus. Hallowed be Thy Name!

I bless You, *Jehovah-Tsidkenu,* my Righteousness. Thank You for becoming sin for me that I might become the righteousness of God in Christ Jesus. Hallowed be Thy Name!

Jehovah-Rohi, You are my Shepherd and I shall not want for any good or beneficial thing. Hallowed be Thy Name!

Hallelujah to *Jehovah-Shammah* Who will never leave or forsake me. You are always there. I take comfort and am encouraged and confidently and boldly say, The Lord is my Helper, I will not be seized with alarm

— I will not fear or dread or be terrified. What can man do to me? Hallowed be Thy Name!

I worship and adore You, *El-Elyon*, the Most High God Who is the First Cause of everything, the Possessor of the heavens and earth. You are the Everlasting-God, the Great-God, the Living-God, the Merciful-God, the Faithful-God, the Mighty-God. You are Truth, Justice, Righteousness, and Perfection. You are *El-Elyon* — the Highest Sovereign of the heavens and the earth. Hallowed be Thy Name!

Father, You have exalted above all else Your Name and Your Word, and You have magnified Your Word above all Your Name! The Word was made flesh, and dwelt among us, and His Name is Jesus! Hallowed be Thy Name!

Scripture References

Matthew 6:9
Psalm 103:1
Genesis 1:1,2
Psalm 8:5b
Genesis 49:24,25
Genesis 15:1,2,8
Hebrews 13:8
Genesis 22:14
Psalm 147:3 AMP
Exodus 15:23-26 AMP
Psalm 107:20
Psalm 103:3
Leviticus 20:7,8
Exodus 17:15

Song of Solomon 2:4
Isaiah 59:19
Judges 6:24
Philippians 4:7 AMP
Jeremiah 23:5,6
2 Corinthians 5:21
Psalm 23:1
Psalm 34:10
Ezekiel 48:35
Hebrews 13:5
Hebrews 13:6 AMP
Psalm 91:1
Psalm 138:2 AMP
John 1:14

8

DIVINE INTERVENTION
"Thy Kingdom Come"

Father, I pray according to Matthew 6:10, Thy Kingdom come. I am looking for the soon coming of our Lord and Savior Jesus Christ.

Today, we are [even here and] now Your children; it is not yet disclosed (made clear) what we shall be [hereafter], *but we know that when He comes and is manifested we shall [as God's children] resemble and be like Him, for we shall see Him just as He [really] is.* You said that everyone who has this hope [resting] on Him cleanses (purifies) himself just as He is pure — chaste, undefiled, guiltless.

For the grace of God — His unmerited favor and blessing — has come forward (appeared) for the deliverance from sin and the eternal salvation for all mankind. It has trained us to reject and renounce all ungodliness (irreligion) and worldly (passionate) desires, to live discreet (temperate, self-controlled), upright, devout (spiritually whole) lives in this present world, awaiting and looking for the [fulfillment, the realization of our] blessed hope, *even the glorious appearing of our great God and Savior Christ Jesus, the Messiah, the Anointed One.*

For the Lord Himself shall descend from heaven with a shout, with the voice of the archangel, and with the trump of God: and the dead in Christ shall rise first. Then we which are alive and remain shall be caught up together with them in the clouds, to meet the Lord in the air: and so shall we ever be with the Lord.

I thank You, Father, that the Lord shall come (to earth), and all the holy ones [saints and angels] with Him; and the Lord shall be King over all the earth; in that day He shall be one Lord, and His name one. The government shall be upon His shoulder.

Father, I thank You that we shall join the great voices in heaven saying, The kingdoms of this world are become the kingdoms of our Lord, and of His Christ; and He shall reign for ever and ever.

Yours, O Lord, is the greatness, and power, and the glory, and the victory, and the majesty; for all that is in the heavens and the earth is Yours; Yours is the Kingdom, O Lord, and Yours it is to be exalted as head over all. Thy Kingdom come. Hallelujah!

Scripture References

1 John 3:2,3 AMP	Isaiah 9:6 AMP
Titus 2:11-13 AMP	Revelation 11:15
1 Thessalonians 4:16,17	1 Chronicles 29:11 AMP
Zechariah 14:5,9 AMP	

9

SUBMISSION
"Thy Will Be Done"

Father, I pray that the will of God be done in my life as it is in heaven. For I am Your [own] handiwork (Your workmanship), recreated in Christ Jesus, [born anew] that I may do those good works which You predestined (planned beforehand) for me, (taking paths which You prepared ahead of time) that I should walk in them — living the good life which You prearranged and made ready for me to live.

Teach me to do Your will, for You are my God; let Your good Spirit lead me into a plain country and into the land of uprightness. Jesus, You gave (yielded) Yourself up [to atone] for my sins (and to save and sanctify me), in order to rescue and deliver me from this present wicked age and world order, in accordance with the will and purpose and plan of our God and Father.

In the name of Jesus, I am not conformed to this world, but am transformed by the renewing of my mind, that I may prove what is that good, and acceptable, and perfect, will of God. For this is the will of God, that I should be consecrated — separated and set apart for pure and holy living: that I should abstain from all sexual vice; that I should know how to possess [control, manage] my own body (in purity, separated from things profane, and) in consecration and honor, not [to be used] in the passion of lust, like the heathen who are ignorant of the true God and have no knowledge of His will.

Father, thank You that You chose me — actually picked me out for Yourself as Your own — in Christ before the foundation of the world; that I should be holy (consecrated and set apart for You) and blameless in Your sight, even above reproach, before You in love: having predestinated me unto the adoption of a child by Jesus Christ to Yourself, according to the good pleasure of Your will.

Your will be done on earth in my life as it is in heaven. Amen and so be it!

Scripture References

Matthew 6:9b,10	Romans 12:2
Ephesians 2:10 AMP	1 Thessalonians 4:4,5 AMP
Psalm 143:10AMP	Ephesians 1:4 AMP
Galatians 1:4 AMP	Ephesians 1:5

10
PROVISION
"Give Us This Day
Our Daily Bread"

In the name of Jesus, I confess with the Psalmist David, I have not seen the righteous forsaken, nor his seed begging bread.

Father, thank You for food, clothing and shelter. In the name of Jesus, I have stopped being perpetually uneasy (anxious and worried) about my life, what I shall eat and what I shall drink, or about my body, what I shall put on. My life is greater [in quality] than food, and the body [far above and more excellent] than clothing.

The bread of idleness [gossip, discontent and self-pity] I will not eat. It is You, Father, Who will liberally supply (fill to the full) my every need according to Your riches in glory in Christ Jesus.

In the name of Jesus, I shall not live by bread alone, but by every word that proceeds from the mouth of God. Your words were found, and I did eat them, and Your Word was to me a joy and the rejoicing of my heart.

And the Word became flesh, and dwelt among us. Jesus, You are the Bread of Life — that gives me life, the Living Bread.

Thank You, Father, in the name of Jesus, for spiritual bread — manna from heaven.

Scripture References

Matthew 6:9b-11

Psalm 37:25

Matthew 6:25 AMP

Proverbs 31:27b AMP

Philippians 4:19 AMP

Matthew 4:4

Jeremiah 15:16 AMP

John 1:14a

John 6:48-51 AMP

11
FORGIVENESS
"Forgive Us Our Debts"

Father, I forgive everyone who has trespassed against me so that You can forgive me my trespasses. [Now, having received the Holy Spirit and being led and directed by Him] if I forgive the sins of anyone they are forgiven; if I retain the sins of anyone, they are retained.

Father, Your Word says, **Love your enemies and pray for those who persecute you** (Matt. 5:44 AMP).

I come before you in Jesus' name to lift _____ before You. I invoke blessings upon him/her and pray for his/her happiness. I implore Your blessings (favor) upon him/her.

Father, not only will I pray for _____, but I set myself to treat him/her well (do good to, act nobly toward) him/her. I will be merciful, sympathetic, tender, responsive, and compassionate toward _____ even as You are, Father.

I am an imitator of You, and I can do all things through Christ Jesus Who strengthens me.

Father, I thank You that I have great peace in this situation, for I love Your law and refuse to take offense toward _____.

Jesus, I am blessed — happy [with life — joy and satisfaction in God's favor and salvation apart from outward conditions] and to be envied — because I take no offense in You and refuse to be hurt or resentful or annoyed or repelled or made to stumble, [whatever may occur].

And now, Father, I roll this work upon You — commit and trust it wholly to You; and believe that You will cause my thoughts to become in agreement to Your will, and so my plans shall be established and succeed.

Scripture References

Matthew 6:12	Ephesians 5:1 AMP
Matthew 6:14,15	Philippians 4:13 AMP
John 20:23 AMP	Psalm 119:165 AMP
Luke 6:27b AMP	Luke 7:23 AMP
Matthew 5:44 AMP	Proverbs 16:3 AMP
Luke 6:28 AMP	

12
GUIDANCE AND DELIVERANCE
"Lead Us Not Into Temptation"

There has no temptation taken me but such as is common to man: but *God is faithful,* Who will not suffer me to be tempted above that which I am able; but will with the temptation also make a way to escape, that I may be able to bear it.

I count it all joy when I fall into various temptations; knowing this, that the trying of my faith works patience.

I will not say when I am tempted, I am tempted from God; for God is incapable of being tempted by [what is] evil and He Himself tempts no one.

Thank You, Jesus, for giving Yourself for my sins, that You might deliver me from this present evil world, according to the will of God and our Father: to Whom be glory for ever and ever.

Father, in the name of Jesus, and according to the power that is at work in me, I will keep awake (give strict attention, be cautious) and watch and pray that I may not come into temptation. In Jesus' name, amen.

Scripture References

1 Corinthians 10:13	Galatians 1:4,5
James 1:2,3	Ephesians 3:20b
James 1:13 AMP	Matthew 26:41a AMP

13

PRAISE

"For Thine Is the Kingdom, and the Power, and the Glory"

O magnify the Lord with me, and let us exalt His name together.

As for God, His way is perfect! The Word of the Lord is tested and tried; He is a shield to all those who take refuge and put their trust in him.

Let the words of my mouth and the meditation of my heart be acceptable in Your sight, O Lord, my firm, impenetrable rock and my redeemer.

Your Word has revived me and given me life.

Forever, O Lord, Your Word is settled in heaven.

Your Word is a lamp to my feet and a light to my path.

The sum of Your Word is truth and every one of Your righteous decrees endures forever.

I will worship toward Your Holy Temple, and praise Your name for Your loving-kindness and for Your truth and faithfulness; for You have exalted above all else Your name and Your Word, and You have magnified Your Word above all Your name!

Let my prayer be set forth as incense before You, the lifting up of my hands as the evening sacrifice. Set a guard, O Lord, before my mouth; keep watch at the door of my lips.

He who brings an offering of praise and thanksgiving honors and glorifies Me; and he who orders his way aright — who prepares the way that I may show him — to him I will demonstrate the salvation of God.

My mouth shall be filled with Your praise and with Your honor all the day.

Because Your loving-kindness is better than life, my lips shall praise You. So will I bless You while I live; I will lift up my hands in Your name.

Your testimonies also are my delight and my counselors.

Scripture References (AMP)

Psalm 34:3	Psalm 138:2
Psalm 18:30	Psalm 142:2,3
Psalm 19:14	Psalm 50:23
Psalm 119:50	Psalm 71:8
Psalm 119:89	Psalm 63,3,4
Psalm 119:105	Psalm 119:24
Psalm 119:160	

14
STRENGTH TO OVERCOME CARES AND BURDENS

Why are you cast down, O my inner self? And why should you moan over me and be disquieted within me?

Father, You set Yourself against the proud and haughty, but give grace [continually] unto the humble. I submit myself therefore to You, God. In the name of Jesus, I resist the devil, and he will flee from me. I resist the cares of the church which try to pressure me daily. Except the Lord builds the house, they labor in vain who build it.

Jesus, I come to You, for I labor and am heavy-laden and over burdened, and You cause me to rest — You will ease and relieve and refresh my soul.

I take Your Yoke upon me, and I learn of You; for You are gentle (meek) and humble (lowly) in heart, and I will find rest — relief, ease and refreshment and recreation and blessed quiet — for my soul. For Your yoke is wholesome *(easy)* — not harsh, hard, sharp or pressing, but comfortable, gracious and pleasant; and Your burden is light and easy to be borne.

I cast my burden on You, Lord, [releasing the weight of it] and You will sustain me; I thank You that You will never allow me, the [consistently] righteous, to be moved — made to slip, fall or fail.

In the name of Jesus, I withstand the devil. I am firm in my faith [against his onset] — rooted, established, strong, immovable and determined. I cease from [the weariness and pain] of human labor; and am zealous and exert myself and strive diligently to enter into the rest [of God] — to know and experience it for myself.

Father, I thank You that Your presence goes with me, and that You give me rest. I am still and rest in You, Lord; I wait for You, and patiently stay myself upon You. I will not fret myself, nor shall I let my heart be troubled, neither shall I let it be afraid. I hope in You, God, and wait expectantly for You; for I shall yet praise You, for You are the help of my countenance, and my God.

Scripture References (AMP)

Psalm 42:11a	Hebrews 4:10b,11
James 4:6,7	Exodus 33:14
Psalm 127:1a	Psalm 37:7
Matthew 11:28-30	John 14:27b
Psalm 55:22	Psalm 42:11b
1 Peter 5:9a	

15
RENEWING THE MIND

Father, I thank You that I shall prosper and be in health, even as my soul prospers. I have the mind of Christ, the Messiah, and do hold the thoughts (feelings and purposes) of His heart. I trust in You, Lord, with all my heart; I lean not unto my own understanding, but in all my ways I acknowledge You, and You shall direct my paths.

Today I submit myself to Your Word which exposes and sifts and analyzes and judges the very thoughts and purposes of my heart. (For the weapons of my warfare are not carnal, but mighty through You to the pulling down of strongholds — *intimidation, fears, doubts, unbelief and failure.*) I refute arguments and theories and reasonings and every proud and lofty thing that sets itself up against the (true) knowledge of God; and I lead every thought and purpose away captive into the obedience of Christ, the Messiah, the Anointed One.

Today I shall be transformed by the renewing of my mind, that I may prove what is that good and acceptable and perfect will of God. Your Word, Lord, shall not depart out of my mouth; but I shall meditate on it day and night, that I may observe to do according to all that is written therein: for then I shall make my way prosperous, then I shall have good success.

My thoughts are the thoughts of the diligent which tend only to plenteousness. Therefore I will not fret or have any anxiety about anything, but in everything by prayer and petition [definite requests] with thanksgiving continue to make my wants known unto You, Lord. And Your peace which transcends all understanding, shall garrison and mount guard over my heart and mind in Christ Jesus.

Today I fix my mind on whatever is *true,* whatever is *worthy* of *reverence* and is *honorable* and *seemly,* whatever is *pure,* whatever is *lovely* and *lovable,* whatever is *kind* and *winsome* and *gracious.* If there is any *virtue* and *excellence,* if there is anything *worthy* of *praise,* I will think on and weigh and take account of these things.

Today I roll my works upon You, Lord — I commit and trust them wholly to You; [You will cause my thoughts to become agreeable to Your will, and] so shall my plans be established and succeed.

Scripture References

3 John 2
1 Corinthians 2:16b AMP
Proverbs 3:5,6
Hebrews 4:12b AMP
2 Corinthians 10:4
2 Corinthians 10:5 AMP

Romans 12:2
Joshua 1:8
Proverbs 21:5a
Philippians 4:6-8 AMP
Proverbs 16:3 AMP

16
CONQUERING THE
THOUGHT LIFE

In the name of Jesus, I take authority over my thought life. Even though I walk (live) in the flesh, I am not carrying on my warfare according to the flesh and using mere human weapons. For the weapons of my warfare are not physical (weapons of flesh and blood), but they are mighty before God for the overthrow and destruction of strongholds. I refute arguments and theories and reasonings and every proud and lofty thing that sets itself up against the (true) knowledge of God; and I lead every thought and purpose away captive into the obedience of Christ, the Messiah, the Anointed One.

With my soul I will bless the Lord with every thought and purpose in life. My mind will not wander out of the presence of God. My life shall glorify the Father — *spirit, soul, and body.* I take no account of the evil done to me — I pay no attention to a suffered wrong. It holds no place in my thought life. I am ever ready to believe the best of every person. I gird up the loins of my mind, and I set my mind and keep it set on what is above — the higher things — not on the things that are on the earth.

Whatever is true, whatever is worthy of reverence and is honorable and seemly, whatever is just, whatever is pure, whatever is lovely and lovable, whatever is kind and winsome and gracious, if there is any virtue and excellence, if there is anything worthy of praise, I will think on and weigh and take account of these things — I will fix my mind on them.

The carnal mind is no longer operative for I have the mind of Christ, the Messiah, and do hold the thoughts (feelings and purposes) of His heart. In the name of Jesus, I will practice what I have learned and received and heard and seen in Christ, and model my way of living on it, and the God of peace — of untroubled, undisturbed well-being — will be with me.

Scripture References (AMP)

2 Corinthians 10:3-5
Psalm 103:1
1 Corinthians 6:20
1 Corinthians 13:5b,7a
1 Peter 1:13

Colossians 3:2
Philippians 4:8
1 Corinthians 2:16
Philippians 4:9

17

GODLY WISDOM IN THE AFFAIRS OF LIFE

Father, You said if anyone lacks wisdom, let him ask of You, Who giveth to all men liberally, and upbraideth not; and it shall be given him. Therefore, I ask in faith, nothing wavering, to be filled with the knowledge of Your will in all wisdom and spiritual understanding. Today I incline my ear unto wisdom, and apply my heart to understanding so that I might receive that which has been freely given unto me.

In the name of Jesus, I receive skill and godly wisdom and instruction. I discern and comprehend the words of understanding and insight. I receive instruction in wise dealing and the discipline of wise thoughtfulness, righteousness, justice, and integrity. Prudence, knowledge, discretion, and discernment are given to me. I increase in knowledge. As a person of understanding, I acquire skill and attain to sound counsels [so that I may be able to steer my course rightly].

Wisdom will keep, defend, and protect me; I love her and she guards me. I prize Wisdom highly and exalt her; she will bring me to honor because I embrace her. She gives to my head a wreath of gracefulness; a crown

62

of beauty and glory will she deliver to me. Length of days is in her right hand, and in her left hand are riches and honor.

Jesus has been made unto me wisdom, and in Him are all the treasures of [divine] wisdom, [of comprehensive insight into the ways and purposes of God], and [all the riches of spiritual] knowledge and enlightenment are stored up and lie hidden. God has hidden away sound and godly wisdom and stored it up for me, for I am the righteousness of God in Christ Jesus.

Therefore, I will walk in paths of uprightness. When I walk, my steps shall not be hampered — my path will be clear and open; and when I run I shall not stumble. I take fast hold of instruction, and do not let her go; I guard her, for she is my life. I let my eyes look right on [with fixed purpose], and my gaze is straight before me. I consider well the path of my feet, and I let all my ways be established and ordered aright.

Father, in the name of Jesus, I look carefully to how I walk! I live purposefully and worthily and accurately, not as unwise and witless, but as a wise — sensible, intelligent person; making the very most of my time — buying up every opportunity.

Scripture References

James 1:5,6a	1 Corinthians 1:30
Colossians 1:9b	Colossians 2:3 AMP
Proverbs 2:2	Proverbs 2:7 AMP
Proverbs 1:2-5 AMP	2 Corinthians 5:21
Proverbs 4:6,8,9 AMP	Proverbs 4:11-13,25,26 AMP
Proverbs 3:16 AMP	Ephesians 5:15,16 AMP

18
HEALING FOR
DAMAGED EMOTIONS

Father, in the name of Jesus, I come to You with a feeling of shame and emotional hurt. I confess my transgressions to You [continually unfolding the past till all is told]. You are faithful and just to forgive me and cleanse me of all unrighteousness. You are my hiding place and You, Lord, preserve me from trouble. You surround me with songs and shouts of deliverance. I have chosen life and according to Your Word You saw me while I was being formed in my Mother's womb and on the authority of Your Word I was wonderfully made. Now, I am Your handiwork, recreated in Christ Jesus.

Father, You have delivered me from the spirit of fear and I shall not be ashamed. Neither shall I be confounded and depressed. You gave me beauty for ashes, the oil of joy for mourning and the garment of praise for the spirit of heaviness that I might be a tree of righteousness, the planting of the Lord, that You might be glorified. I speak out in psalms, hymns and spiritual songs, offering praise with my voice and making melody with all my heart to the Lord. Just as David did in 1 Samuel 30:6 I encourage myself in the Lord.

I believe in God Who raised Jesus from the dead, Who was betrayed and put to death because of my misdeeds and was raised to secure my acquittal, absolving me from all guilt before God. Father, You anointed Jesus and sent Him to bind up and heal my broken heart, and liberate me from the shame of my youth and the imperfections of my caretakers. In the name of Jesus, I choose to forgive all those who have wronged me in any way. You will not leave me without support as I complete the forgiveness process. I take comfort and am encouraged and confidently say, "The Lord is my Helper; I will not be seized with alarm. What can man do to me?"

My spirit is the candle of the Lord searching all the innermost parts of my being and the Holy Spirit leads me into all truth. When reality exposes shame and emotional pain, I remember that the sufferings of this present life are not worth being compared with the glory that is about to be revealed to me and in me and for me and conferred on me! The chastisement needful to obtain my peace and well-being was upon Jesus, and with the stripes that wounded Him I was healed and made whole. As Your child, Father, I have a joyful and confident hope of eternal salvation. This hope will never disappoint, delude or shame me, for God's love has been poured out in my heart through the Holy Spirit Who has been given to me.

Scripture References

Psalm 32:5-7 AMP	Romans 4:24,25
1 John 1:9	Isaiah 61:1
Deuteronomy 30:19	Mark 11:25
Psalm 139	Hebrews 13:5,6
Ephesians 2:10	Proverbs 20:27
2 Timothy 1:7	John 16:13
Isaiah 54:4	Romans 8:18
Isaiah 61:3	Isaiah 53:5b
Ephesians 5:19	Romans 5:3-5

19
THE SETTING OF PROPER PRIORITIES

Father, in the name of Jesus, I come before You. Spirit of Truth, Who comes from the Father, it is You Who guides me into all truth. According to 3 John 2 it is God's will that I prosper in every way and that my body keeps well, even as my soul keeps well and prospers.

One thing I ask of You, Lord, one thing will I seek after, inquire for and [insistently] require, that I may dwell in Your house [in Your presence], all the days of my life, to behold and gaze upon Your beauty. I come to meditate, consider and inquire in Your temple *(about success in life)*.

Father, You have said, **I will not in any way fail you nor give you up nor leave you without support. [I will] not, [I will] not, [I will] not in any degree leave you helpless, nor forsake nor let [you] down, [relax my hold on you]. — Assuredly not** (Heb. 13:5 AMP)! So I take comfort and am encouraged and confidently and boldly say that the Lord is my Helper, I will not be seized with alarm — I will not fear or dread or be terrified. What can man do to me?

In the name of Jesus, I am strong and very courageous, that I may do according to all Your Word. I turn not from it to the right hand or to the left, that I may prosper wherever I go. The Word of God shall not depart out of my mouth, but I shall meditate on it day and night. I hear therefore and am watchful to keep the instructions, the laws and precepts of my Lord God, that it may be well with me and that I may increase exceedingly, as the Lord God has promised me, in a land flowing with milk and honey. The Lord my God is one Lord — the only Lord. And I shall love the Lord my God with all my [mind and] heart, and with my entire being, and with all my might. And I will love my neighbor as myself.

Jesus, You said that when I do this I will live — enjoy active, blessed, endless life in the Kingdom of God. Therefore, I will not worry or be anxious about what I am going to eat, or what I am going to have to drink, or what I am going to have to wear. My heavenly Father knows that I need them all. But I purpose in my heart to seek for (aim at and strive after) first of all Your Kingdom, Lord, and Your righteousness [Your way of doing and being right], and then all these things taken together will be given me besides.

Now thanks be to You, Father, Who always causes me to triumph in Christ!

Scripture References

John 16:13a	Deuteronomy 6:1,3-5 AMP
Psalm 27:4 AMP	Luke 10:27,28 AMP
Hebrews 13:5b,6 AMP	Matthew 6:31-33 AMP
Joshua 1:7,8a AMP	2 Corinthians 2:14

20
BEING EQUIPPED
FOR SUCCESS

Father, I thank You that the entrance of Your words gives light. I thank You that Your Word which You speak *(and which I speak)* is alive and full of power — making it active, operative, energizing, and effective. I thank You, Father, that [You have given me a spirit] of power, and of love, and of a calm and well-balanced mind, and discipline, and self-control. I have Your power and ability and sufficiency, for You have qualified me (making me to be fit and worthy and sufficient) as a minister and dispenser of a new covenant [of salvation through Christ].

In the name of Jesus, I walk out of the realm of failure into the arena of success, giving thanks to You, Father, for You have qualified and made me fit to share the portion which is the inheritance of the saints (God's holy people) in the Light.

Father, You have delivered and drawn me to Yourself out of the control and the dominion of darkness *(failure, doubt and fear)* and have transferred me into the Kingdom of the Son of Your love, in Whom there is good success [and freedom from fears, agitating passions, and moral conflicts]. I rejoice in Jesus Who has come that I might have life and have it more abundantly.

Today I am a new creation, for I am (ingrafted) in Christ, the Messiah. The old (previous moral and spiritual condition) has passed away. Behold, the fresh and new has come! I forget those things which are behind me and reach forth unto those things which are before me. I am crucified with Christ: nevertheless I live; yet not I, but Christ lives in me: and the life which I now live in the flesh I live by the faith of the Son of God, Who loved me, and gave Himself for me.

Today I attend to the Word of God. I consent and submit to Your sayings, Father. Your words shall not depart from my sight; I will keep them in the midst of my heart. For they are life *(success)* to me, healing and health to all my flesh. I keep my heart with all vigilance and above all that I guard, for out of it flow the springs of life.

Today I will not let mercy and kindness and truth forsake me. I bind them about my neck; I write them upon the tablet of my heart. So therefore I will find favor, good understanding, and high esteem in the sight [or judgment] of God and man.

Today my delight and desire are in the law of the Lord, and on His law I habitually meditate (ponder and study) by day and by night. Therefore I am like a tree firmly planted [and tended] by the streams of water, ready to bring forth my fruit in my season; my leaf also shall not fade or wither, and everything I do shall prosper [and come to maturity].

Now thanks be to God, Who always causes me to triumph in Christ!

Scripture References

Psalm 119:130
Hebrews 4:12a AMP
2 Timothy 1:7b AMP
2 Corinthians 3:5b-6a AMP
Colossians 1:12,13 AMP
2 Corinthians 1:12,13 AMP
2 Corinthians 5:17 AMP

John 10:10b AMP
Philippians 3:13b
Galatians 2:20
Proverbs 4:20-23 AMP
Proverbs 3:3,4 AMP
Psalm 1:2,3 AMP
2 Corinthians 2:14

21
PRAYER FOR THE SUCCESS
OF A BUSINESS

Father, Your Word says that I am a partaker of the inheritance and treasures of heaven. You have delivered me out of the authority of darkness and translated me into the kingdom of Your dear Son. Father, where Your Word is there is light and, also, understanding. Your Word does not return to You void but always accomplishes what it is sent to do. I am a joint-heir with Jesus and as Your son/daughter, I accept that the communication of my faith is effectual by the acknowledging of every good work which is in me in Christ Jesus.

Father, I commit my works (the plans and cares of my business) to You, entrust them wholly to You. Since You are effectually at work in me, You cause my thoughts to become agreeable with Your will, so that my business plans shall be established and succeed. In the name of Jesus, I submit to every kind of wisdom, practical insight and prudence which You have lavished upon me in accordance with the riches and generosity of Your gracious favor.

Father, I affirm that I obey Your Word by making an honest living with my own hands so that I may be able to give to those in need. In Your strength and according to Your grace I provide for myself and my own family. Thank You, Father, for making all grace, every favor and earthly blessing come to me in abundance that I, having all sufficiency, may abound to every good work.

Father, thank You for the ministering spirits that You have assigned to go forth to bring in consumers. Jesus said, "You are the light of the world." In His Name my light shall so shine before all men that they may see my good works glorifying You, my heavenly Father.

Thank You for the grace to remain diligent in seeking knowledge and skill in areas where I am inexperienced. I ask You for wisdom and the ability to understand righteousness, justice, and fair dealing in every area and relationship. I affirm that I am faithful and committed to Your Word. My life and business are founded upon its principles.

Father, thank You for the success of my business!

Scripture References

Romans 8:17	1 Timothy 5:8
Colossians 1:12	2 Corinthians 9:8
Psalm 119:130	Hebrews 1:14
Philemon 1:6	Matthew 5:14,16
Proverbs 16:3	Proverbs 22:29
Philippians 2:13	Proverbs 2:9
Ephesians 1:7,8	Proverbs 4:20-22
Ephesians 4:28	

22

KNOWING GOD'S WILL

Father, I thank You that You are instructing me in the way which I should go and that You are guiding me with Your eye. I thank You for Your guidance and leading concerning Your will, Your plan, and Your purpose for my life. I do hear the voice of the Good Shepherd, for I know You and follow You. You lead me in the paths of righteousness for Your name's sake.

Thank You, Father, that my path is growing brighter and brighter until it reaches the full light of day. As I follow You, Lord, I believe my path is becoming clearer each day.

Thank You, Father, that Jesus was made unto me wisdom. Confusion is not a part of my life. I am not confused about Your will for my life. I trust in You and lean not unto my own understanding. As I acknowledge You in all my ways, You are directing my paths. I believe that as I trust in You completely, You will show me the path of life.

Scripture References

Psalm 32:8
John 10:3,4
Psalm 23:3
Proverbs 4:18
Ephesians 5:19

1 Corinthians 1:30
1 Corinthians 14:33
Proverbs 3:5,6
Psalm 16:11

23

PEACEFUL SLEEP

In the name of Jesus, I bind you, Satan, and all your agents from my dreams. I forbid you to interfere in any way with my sleep.

I bring every thought, every imagination, and every dream into the captivity and obedience of Jesus Christ. Father, I thank You that even as I sleep my heart counsels me and reveals to me Your purpose and plan. Thank You for sweet sleep, for You promised Your beloved sweet sleep. Therefore, my heart is glad, and my spirit rejoices. My body and soul rest and confidently dwell in safety.

Scripture References

Matthew 16:19   Psalm 16:7-9
Matthew 18:18   Psalm 127:2
2 Corinthians 10:5   Proverbs 3:24

24
VICTORY OVER PRIDE

Father, Your Word says that You hate a proud look, that You resist the proud but give grace to the humble. I submit myself therefore to You, God. In the name of Jesus, I resist the devil, and he will flee from me. I renounce every manifestation of pride in my life as sin; I repent and turn from it.

As an act of faith, I clothe myself with humility and receive Your grace. I humble myself under Your mighty hand, Lord, that You may exalt me in due time. I refuse to exalt myself. I do not think of myself more highly than I ought; I do not have an exaggerated opinion of my own importance, but rate my ability with sober judgment, according to the degree of faith apportioned to me.

Proverbs 11:2 says, **When pride cometh, then cometh shame: but with the lowly is wisdom.** Father, I set myself to resist pride when it comes. My desire is to be counted among the lowly, so I take on the attitude of a servant.

Father, thank You that You dwell with him who is of a contrite and humble spirit. You revive the spirit of the humble and revive the heart of the contrite ones. Thank You that the reward of humility and the reverent

and worshipful fear of the Lord is riches and honor
and life.

Scripture References

Proverbs 6:16   Proverbs 11:2
James 4:6,7   Matthew 23:11
Proverbs 21:4   Isaiah 57:15
1 Peter 5:5,6   Proverbs 22:4 AMP
Romans 12:3 AMP

25

OVERCOMING INTIMIDATION

Father, I come to You in the name of Jesus, confessing that intimidation has caused me to stumble. I ask Your forgiveness for thinking of myself as inferior, for I am created in your image, and I am Your workmanship. Jesus said that the Kingdom of God is in me. Therefore, the power that raised Jesus from the dead dwells in me and causes me to face life with hope and divine energy.

The Lord is my light and my salvation; whom shall I fear? The Lord is the strength of my life; of whom shall I be afraid? Lord, You said that You would never leave me or forsake me. Therefore, I can say without any doubt or fear that You are my helper, and I am not afraid of anything that mere man can do to me. Greater is He Who is in me than he who is in the world. If God is for me, who can be against me? I am free from the fear of man and public opinion.

Father, You have not given me a spirit of timidity — of cowardice, of craven and cringing and fawning fear — but You have given me a spirit of power and of love and of a calm and well-balanced mind and discipline and self-control. I can do all things through Christ who gives me the strength.

Scripture References (AMP)

1 John 1:9	Ephesians 2:10
Luke 17:21	Ephesians 1:19,20
Colossians 1:29	Psalm 1:27
Hebrews 13:5	1 John 4:4
Romans 3:31	Proverbs 29:25
2 Timothy 1:7	Philippians 4:13

26
PROTECTION FOR TRAVEL

Father, today I confess Your Word over my travel plans and know that Your Word does not go out and return to You void, but it accomplishes what You say it will do. I give You thanks for moving quickly to perform Your Word and fulfill its promises.

As I prepare to travel, I rejoice in the promises that Your Word holds for protection and safety of the righteous. Only You, Father, make me live in safety. I trust in You and dwell in Your protection. If I shall face any problems or trouble, I will run to You, Father, my strong tower and shelter in time of need. Believing in the written Word of God, I speak peace, safety and success over my travel plans, in Jesus' name.

As a child of God, my path of travel is preserved and angels keep charge over me and surround my car/airplane/ship. I will proceed with my travel plans without fear of accidents, problems or any type of frustrations. I have the peace of God and will allow fear no place as I travel; the Lord delivers me from every type of evil and preserves me for His kingdom. I stand confident that my travel plans will not be disrupted or confused.

Thank You, Father, that in every situation You are there to protect me. No matter in what means of transportation I choose to travel, You have redeemed me and will protect me. The earth and all things on it are under Your command. You are my Heavenly Father. Through my faith in You, I have the power to tread on serpents and have all power over the enemy. No food or water will harm me when I arrive at my destination. My travel is safe.

Father, I give You the glory in this situation. Thank You that as I keep Your ways before me, I will be safe. Your mercy is upon me and my family, and our travels will be safe. Not a hair on our heads shall perish. Thank You, Father, for Your guidance and safety — You are worthy of all praise!

Scripture References

Isaiah 55:11

Jeremiah 1:12

Psalm 4:8

Psalm 91:1

Proverbs 18:10

Proverbs 29:25

Mark 11:23,24

Proverbs 2:8

Psalm 91:11,12

2 Timothy 4:18

Philippians 4:7

2 Timothy 1:7

Isaiah 43:1-3

2 Timothy 4:18

Hosea 2:18

Luke 10:19

Psalm 91:13

Luke 21:18

Mark 16:18

Matthew 18:18

John 14:13

Daniel 9:18

Luke 1:50

27

THE NEW CREATION MARRIAGE

Introduction*

The harmony and unity in a church will never exceed the harmony and unity in the homes represented in the congregation. Each household actually should be a mini-church coming together to form a body of believers. Love must originate from God the Father. For years I gave glory to the Lord for the love and peace of God which reigned supreme in our home. Many times circumstances said, "It isn't so"; God, however, watched over His Word to perform it in our lives.

You become a doer of the Word in your own home by obeying the Royal Law of Love. God is looking within each family for one intercessor who will "stand in the gap" and "put up a hedge" for the entire household. I encourage you to be that one who makes the decision to be subject to God for the purpose of peace, harmony, and unity. Stand firm against the devil: resist him, and he will flee from your family.

---

*Germaine Copeland's introduction to this prayer.

The following prayer was given to me by the Holy Spirit for my husband and me.

Husband, you may pray the part for the wife in the third person.

Wife, you may pray the part for the husband in the third person.

Find time to pray together, if both parties are willing and receptive.

Prayer

The couple prays together:

Father, in the name of Jesus, we rejoice and delight ourselves in one another. We are in Christ, the Messiah, and have become (new creatures altogether), new creations; the old (previous moral and spiritual condition) has passed away. Behold, the fresh and new has come! May our family be seen as bright lights — stars or beacons shining out clearly — in the [dark] world.

The husband prays:

I love my wife, as Christ loves the Church. I am to her what Christ is to the Church. I have given myself up for her, so that I might set her apart for myself, having cleansed her by the washing of water with the Word through intercession and counsel, that I might present her to myself in glorious splendor, for she is [the expression of] my glory (majesty, pre-eminence). Therefore, she is without spot or wrinkle or any such things — but she is holy and faultless as my help meet. I love her as [being in a sense] my own body, for I love her as I love myself. I nourish and carefully protect and cherish her, as Christ does the Church, for we are members (parts) of His body. Jesus is my example. I trust [myself and everything] to God Who judges fairly.

I thank You, Father, that my wife and I are able ministers of the New Covenant — ministers of reconciliation. Father, [in Your love] You chose us — actually picked us out for Yourself as Your own — in Christ before the foundation of the world; that we should be holy (consecrated and set apart for Yourself) before You in love.

Father, my wife and I have received Your favor and mercy which You have lavished upon us in every kind of wisdom and understanding (practical insight and prudence).

The wife prays:

Father, in the name of Jesus, I am submissive — I submit and adapt myself — to my own husband as [a service] to the Lord. I see that I respect and reverence my husband — that I notice him, regard him, honor him, prefer him, venerate and esteem him; and that I defer to him, praise him, and love and admire him exceedingly. The heart of my husband can trust in me confidently and rely on and believe in me safely, so that he has no lack of honest gain or need of dishonest spoil. I will comfort, encourage and do him only good as long as there is life within me.

As I seek counsel from my husband, he will be my strength, my hiding place, my high tower, my intercessor — and we will stand side by side as we minister life, love, healing — soundness and wholeness

— to those God sends our way. We will stand together as one before the Body of Christ.

Scripture References

2 Corinthians 5:17 AMP
Philippians 2:15b AMP
Ephesians 5:25-30 AMP
1 Peter 2:23b AMP
2 Corinthians 3:6
2 Corinthians 5:18

Ephesians 1:4,6,8 AMP
Ephesians 5:22,33b AMP
1 Corinthians 11:7b AMP
Proverbs 31:11,12 AMP
Matthew 19:5,6 AMP

28

WHEN DESIRING
TO HAVE A BABY

Our Father, my spouse and I bow our knees unto You. Father of our Lord Jesus Christ of whom the whole family in heaven and on earth is named, we pray that you would grant to us according to the riches of Your glory, to be strengthened with might by Your Spirit in the inner man. Christ dwells in our hearts by faith, that we — being rooted and grounded in love — may be able to comprehend with all the saints what is the breadth, and length, and depth, and height of the love of Christ, which passes knowledge, that we might be filled with all the fullness of God.

Hallelujah, we praise You, O Lord, for You give children to the childless wife, so that she becomes a happy mother. And we thank You that You are the One who is building our family. As Your children and inheritors through Jesus Christ, we receive Your gift — the fruit of the womb, Your child as our reward.

We praise You, our Father, in Jesus' name, for we know that whatsoever we ask, we receive of You, because we keep Your commandments, and do those things which are pleasing in Your sight.

Prayers That Avail Much — Volume II

Thank You, Father, that we are a fruitful vine within our house; our children will be like olive shoots around our table. Thus shall we be blessed because we fear the Lord.

Scripture References

Ephesians 3:14-19
Psalm 113:9 AMP
Psalm 127:3

1 John 3:22,23 AMP
Psalm 128:3,4 AMP

88

29
THE UNBORN CHILD

Father, I thank You for my unborn child. I treasure this child as a gift from You. My child was created in Your image, perfectly healthy and complete. You have known my child since conception and know the path he/she will take with his/her life. I ask Your blessing upon him/her and stand and believe in his/her salvation through Jesus Christ.

When You created man and woman, You called them blessed and crowned them with glory and honor. It is in You, Father, that my child will live and move, and have his/her being. He/she is Your offspring and will come to worship and praise You.

Heavenly Father, I thank and praise You for the great things You have done and are continuing to do. I am in awe at the miracle of life You have placed inside of me. Thank You!

Scripture References

Psalm 127:3	Matthew 18:18
Genesis 1:26	John 14:13
Jeremiah 1:5	Galatians 3:13
2 Peter 3:9	1 John 3:8
Psalm 8:5	Psalm 91:1
Acts 17:28,29	

30

GODLY ORDER IN PREGNANCY AND CHILDBIRTH

Father, I confess Your Word this day over my pregnancy and the birth of my child. I ask that You will quickly perform Your Word trusting that it will not go out from You and return to You void, but rather that it will accomplish that which pleases You. Your Word is quick and powerful, and discerns my heart intentions and the thoughts of my mind.

Right now I put on the whole armor of God so that I may be able to stand against the tricks and traps of the devil. I recognize that my fight is not with flesh and blood, but against principalities, powers and the rulers of darkness and spiritual wickedness in high places. God, I stand above all, taking the shield of faith and being able to quench the attacks of the devil with Your mighty power. I stand in faith during this pregnancy and birth, not giving any room to fear, but possessing power, love and a sound mind as Your Word promises in 2 Timothy 1:7.

Heavenly Father, I confess that You are my refuge; I trust You during this pregnancy and childbirth. I am thankful that You have put angels at watch over me and my unborn child. I cast all the care and burden of this pregnancy over on You, Lord. Your grace is sufficient for me through this pregnancy; You strengthen my weaknesses.

Father, Your Word declares that my unborn child was created in Your image, fearfully and wonderfully made to praise You. You have made me a joyful mother, and I am blessed with a heritage from You as my reward. I commit this child to You, Father, and pray that he will grow and call me blessed.

I am not afraid of pregnancy or childbirth because I am fixed and trusting upon You, Father. I believe that my pregnancy and childbirth will be void of all problems. Thank You, Father, that all decisions regarding my pregnancy and delivery will be godly, that the Holy Spirit will intervene. Lord, You are my dwelling place and I rest in the knowledge that evil will not come near me and no sickness or infirmity will strike me or my unborn child. I know that Jesus died on the cross to take away my sickness and pain. Having accepted Your Son Jesus as my Savior, I confess that my child will be born healthy and completely whole. Thank You, Father, for the law of the Spirit of life in Christ Jesus that has made me and my child free from the law of sin and death!

Father, thank You for protecting me and my baby and for our good health. Thank You for hearing and answering my prayers.

Scripture References

Jeremiah 1:12	Proverbs 31:28
Isaiah 55:11	Psalm 112:7
Hebrews 4:12	Psalm 91:1,10
Ephesians 6:11,12,16	Matthew 8:17
Psalm 91:2,11	Romans 8:2
1 Peter 5:7	James 4:7
2 Corinthians 12:9	Ephesians 6:12
Genesis 1:26	John 4:13
Psalm 139:14	Matthew 18:18
Psalm 113:9	Jeremiah 33:3
Psalm 127:3	

31
PEACE IN THE FAMILY

Father, in the name of Jesus, I thank You that You have poured Your Spirit upon our family from on high. Our wilderness has become a fruitful field, and we value our fruitful field as a forest. Justice dwells in our wilderness, and righteousness [religious and moral rectitude in every area and relation] abides in our fruitful field. The effect of righteousness is peace [internal and external], and the result of righteousness, quietness and confident trust forever.

Our family dwells in a peaceable habitation, in safe dwellings and in quiet resting places. And there is stability in our times, abundance of salvation, wisdom and knowledge. There reverent fear and worship of the Lord is our treasure and Yours.

O Lord, be gracious to us; we have waited [expectantly] for You. Be the arm of Your servants — our strength and defense — every morning, our salvation in the time of trouble.

Father, we thank You for our peace, our safety and our welfare this day. Hallelujah!

Scripture References (AMP)

Isaiah 32:15-18   Isaiah 33:2,6

PART II
INTERCESSORY PRAYERS
FOR OTHERS

32
REVIVAL

Father, in the name of Jesus, You have revived us again that Your people may rejoice in You. Thank You for showing us Your mercy and lovingkindness, O Lord, and for granting us Your salvation. You have created in us a clean heart, O God, and renewed a right, persevering and steadfast spirit within us. You have restored unto us the joy of Your salvation, and You are upholding us with a willing spirit. Now we will teach transgressors Your ways, and sinners shall be converted and return to You.

We therefore cleanse our ways by taking heed and keeping watch [on ourselves] according to Your Word [conforming our lives to it]. Since Your [great] promises are ours, we cleanse ourselves from everything that contaminates and defiles our bodies and spirits, and bring [our] consecration to completeness in the (reverential) fear of God. With our whole hearts have we sought You, inquiring for You and of You, and yearning for You; O let us not wander or step aside [either in ignorance or willfully] from Your commandments. Your Word have we laid up in our hearts, that we might not sin against You.

Jesus, thank You for cleansing us through the Word — the teachings — which You have given us.

We delight ourselves in Your statutes; we will not forget Your Word. Deal bountifully with Your servants, that we may live; and we will observe Your Word [hearing, receiving, loving, and obeying it].

Father, in the name of Jesus, we are doers of the Word, and not merely listeners to it. It is You, O Most High, Who has revived and stimulated us according to Your Word! Thank You for turning away our eyes from beholding vanity [idols and idolatry]; and restoring us to vigorous life and health in Your ways. Behold, we long for Your precepts; in Your righteousness give us renewed life. This is our comfort and consolation in our affliction, that Your Word has revived us and given us life.

We strip ourselves of our former natures — put off and discard our old unrenewed selves — which characterized our previous manner of life. We are constantly renewed in the spirit of our minds — having a fresh mental and spiritual attitude; and we put on the new nature (the regenerate self) created in God's image, (Godlike) in true righteousness and holiness. Though our outer man is (progressively) decaying and wasting away, our inner self is being (progressively) renewed day after day. Hallelujah!

Scripture References (AMP)

Psalm 85:6,7	James 1:22
Psalm 51:10,12,13	Psalm 119:25
Psalm 119:9-11	Psalm 119:37,40,50
2 Corinthians 7:1	Ephesians 4:22-24
John 15:3	2 Corinthians 4:16b
Psalm 119:16,17	

33
UNITY AND HARMONY

Father, in the name of Jesus, this is the confidence that we have in You, that, if we ask anything according to Your will, You hear us: and since we know that You hear us, whatsoever we ask, we know that we have the petitions that we desire of You.

Father, You said, **Behold, they are of one people, and they have all one language; and this is only the beginning of what they will do; and now nothing they have imagined they can do will be impossible to them** (Gen. 11:6 AMP). We pray by the name of our Lord Jesus, that all of us in Your Body be in perfect harmony, and full agreement in what we say, and that there be no dissensions or factions or divisions among us; but that we be perfectly united in our common understanding and in our opinions and judgments.

Holy Spirit, teach us how to agree (harmonize together, together make a symphony) about — anything and everything — so that whatever we ask will come to pass and be done for us by our Father in heaven.

We pray that as members of the Body of Christ we will live as becomes us — with complete lowliness of mind (humility) and meekness (unselfishness, gentleness, mildness), with patience, bearing with one another and making allowances because we love one another. In the name of Jesus, we are eager and strive earnestly to guard and keep the harmony and oneness of [produced by] the Spirit in the binding power of peace.

We commit, in the name of Jesus, and according to the power of God at work in us, to be of one and the same mind (united in spirit), sympathizing [with one another], loving [each the others] as brethren (of one household), compassionate and courteous — tenderhearted and humble-minded. We will never return evil for evil or insult for insult — scolding, tongue-lashing, berating; but on the contrary blessing — praying for their welfare, happiness, and protection, and truly pitying and loving one another. For we know that to this we have been called, that we may ourselves inherit a blessing [from God] — obtain a blessing as heirs, bringing welfare and happiness and protection.

Father, thank You that Jesus has given to us the glory and honor which You gave Him, that we may be one, [even] as You and Jesus are one: Jesus in us and You in Jesus, in order that we may become one and perfectly united, that the world may know and [definitely] recognize that You sent Jesus, and that You have loved them [even] as You have loved Jesus.

Father, Thy will be done in earth, as it is in heaven. Amen, and so be it.

Scripture References

1 John 5:14,15	Ephesians 4:2,3 AMP
Genesis 11:6 AMP	1 Peter 3:8,9 AMP
1 Corinthians 1:10 AMP	John 17:22,23 AMP
Matthew 18:19 AMP	Matthew 6:10b

34

CHURCH TEACHERS

Father, we come in the Name of Jesus, asking You for called teachers for our classes and choirs. We thank You for teachers who are filled with the Spirit of God, in wisdom and ability, in understanding and intelligence, in knowledge, and in all kinds of craftsmanship, to devise skillful methods for teaching us and our children the Word of God. They are teachers who give themselves to teaching.

Father, may these teachers recognize that they must assume the greater accountability. According to Your Word, teachers will be judged by a higher standard and with greater severity [than other people]. We thank You that our teachers will not offend in speech — never say the wrong things — that they may be fully developed characters and perfect men and women, each one able to control his/her own body and to curb his/her entire nature.

Thank You that our teachers are part of the fivefold ministry who are perfecting and fully equipping the saints (God's consecrated people), [that they should do] the work of ministering toward building up Christ's Body (the church), [that it might develop] until we all attain oneness in the faith and in the comprehension of the full and accurate knowledge of the Son of God; that [we might arrive] at really mature manhood — the completeness of personality which is nothing less than the standard height of Christ's own perfection — the measure of the stature of the fullness of the Christ, and the completeness found in Him.

Thank You, Father, that Your people at our church are no longer children, tossed [like ships] to and fro.

They are enfolded in love, growing up in every way and in all things into Him, Who is the head, [even] Christ, the Messiah, the Anointed One.

Father, You are effectually at work in our teachers — energizing and creating in them the power and desire — both to will and to work for Your good pleasure and satisfaction and delight. Father, in the name of Jesus, their power and ability and sufficiency are from You. [It is You] Who have qualified them (making them to be fit, worthy and sufficient) as ministers and dispensers of a New Covenant. They are not ministers of the law which kills, but of the (Holy) Spirit which makes alive.

Father, we rejoice in the Lord over our teachers and commit to undergird them with our faith and love. We will not judge or criticize them, but speak excellent and princely things concerning them. The opening of our lips shall be for right things.

Thank You, Father, that the teachers live in harmony, with the other members of our church, being in full accord and of one harmonious mind and intention. Each is not [merely] concerned for his/her own interests, but each for the interest of others. Jesus is our example in humility, and our teachers shall tend — nurture, guard, guide, and fold — the flock of God which is [their responsibility], and will be examples of Christian living to the flock (the congregation).

Thank You, Father, for the performance of Your Word in our midst, in the name of Jesus.

Scripture References (AMP)

Exodus 31:3,4	2 Corinthians 3:5b,6
Romans 12:7	Proverbs 8:6
James 3:1,2	Philippians 2:2,4,5
Ephesians 4:12-15	1 Peter 5:2,3
Philippians 2:13	Jeremiah 1:12

35

SUCCESS OF A CONFERENCE

Father, we pray that those who hear the messages at the _____ conference will believe — adhere to and trust in and rely on Jesus as the Christ, and that all those You have called to attend the conference will be there and receive what You have for them.

Let it be known and understood by all that it is in the name and through the power and authority of Jesus Christ of Nazareth, and by means of Him that this conference is successful.

The speakers shall be filled with and controlled by the Holy Spirit. When the people see the boldness and unfettered eloquence of the speakers, they shall marvel and recognize that they have been with Jesus. Everybody shall be praising and glorifying God for what shall be occuring. By the hands of the ministers, numerous and startling signs and wonders will be performed among the people.

Father, in the name of Jesus, we thank You that You have observed the enemy's threats and have granted us, Your bondservants, full freedom to declare Your message fearlessly — while You stretch out Your hand to cure and perform signs and wonders through the authority and by the power of the name of Your Holy Child and Servant Jesus.

We thank You, Father, that when we pray, the place in which we are assembled will be shaken; and we shall all be filled with the Holy Spirit, and Your people shall continue to speak the Word of God with freedom and boldness and courage.

By common consent, we shall all meet together at the conference. More and more individuals shall join themselves with us — a crowd of both men and women. The people shall gather from the north, south, east, and west, bringing the sick and those troubled with foul spirits, and they shall all be cured.

Thank You, Father, that our speakers are men and women of good and attested character and repute, full of the Holy Spirit and wisdom. The people who shall hear will not be able to resist the intelligence and the wisdom and the inspiration of the Spirit with which they speak, in the name of Jesus.

Thank You, Father, for the performance of Your Word in the name of Jesus!

Scripture References (AMP)

Acts 4:10,13,21	Acts 5:12b,13,16
Acts 5:12a	Acts 6:3,10
Acts 4:29-31	

36

VISION FOR A CHURCH

Father, in the name of Jesus, we come into Your presence thanking You for _____ (name of church). You have called us to be saints _____ in _____ (name of city) and around the world. As we lift our voices in one accord, we recognize that You are God, and everything was made by and for You. We call into being those things that be not as though they were.

We thank You that we all speak the same thing: there is no division among us; we are perfectly joined together in the same mind. Grant unto us, Your representatives here, a boldness to speak Your Word which You will confirm with signs following. We thank You that we have workmen in abundance and all manner of cunning people for every manner of work. Each department operates in the excellence of ministry and intercessions. We have in our church the ministry gifts for the edifying of this body till we all come into the unity of the faith, and the knowledge of the Son of God, unto a mature person. None of our people will be children, tossed to and fro, and carried about with every wind of doctrine. We speak the truth in love.

We are a growing and witnessing body of believers becoming _____ (number) strong. We have every need met. Therefore, we meet the needs of people who come — spirit, soul, and body. We ask for the wisdom of God in meeting these needs. Father, we thank You for the ministry facilities that will more than meet the needs of the ministry You have called us to. Our church is prospering financially, and we have more than enough to meet every situation. We have everything we need to carry out Your Great Commission and reach the _____(name of city or county) area for Jesus. We are a people of love as love is shed abroad in our hearts by the Holy Spirit. We thank You that the Word of God is living big in all of us and Jesus is Lord!

We are a supernatural church, composed of supernatural people doing supernatural things, for we are laborers together with God. We thank You for Your presence among us and we lift our hands and praise Your Holy Name!

Scripture References

Acts 4:24	Ephesians 4:11-15
Romans 4:17	Philippians 4:19
1 Corinthians 1:10	Romans 5:5
Acts 4:29	1 Corinthians 3:9
Mark 16:20b	Psalm 63:4
Exodus 35:33	

This prayer was written by and used with the permission of T. R. King; Valley Christian Center; Roanoke, Virginia.

37

PERSONAL PRAYER OF A PASTOR FOR THE CONGREGATION

Father, as the pastor of _____, I approach the throne of grace on behalf of the membership. I thank my God in all my remembrance of them. In every prayer of mine I always make my entreaty and petition for them all with joy (delight). [I thank my God] for their fellowship — their sympathetic co-operation and contributions and partnership — in advancing the good news (the Gospel). And I am convinced and sure of this very thing, that You have begun a good work in them and will continue until the day of Jesus Christ — right up to the time of His return — developing [that good work] and perfecting and bringing it to full completion in them.

In the name of Jesus, it is right and appropriate for me to have this confidence and feel this way about them all, because even as they do me, I hold them in my heart as partakers and sharers, one and all with me, of grace (God's unmerited favor and spiritual blessing).

Father, You are my witness and know how I long for and pursue them all with love, in the tender mercies of Christ Jesus [Himself]!

And this I pray, that their love may abound yet more and more and extend to its fullest development in knowledge and all keen insight — that is, that their love may [display itself in] greater depth of acquaintance and more comprehensive discernment; so that they may surely learn to sense what is vital, and approve and prize what is excellent and of real value — recognizing the highest and best, and distinguishing the moral difference. I pray that they may be untainted and pure and unerring and blameless, that — with hearts sincere and certain and unsullied — they may [approach] the day of Christ, not stumbling nor causing others to stumble.

Father, may the membership abound in and be filled with the fruits of righteousness (of right standing with God and right doing) which comes through Jesus Christ, the Anointed One, to the honor and praise of God — that Your glory may be both manifested and recognized.

I commit myself to You, Father, anew and to them, for I am convinced of this, I shall remain and stay by them all, to promote their progress and joy in believing, so that in me they may have abundant cause for exultation and glorifying in Christ Jesus. In the name of Jesus, they will be sure as citizens so to conduct themselves that their manner of life will be worthy of the good news (the Gospel) of Christ.

Thank You, Father, that they are standing firm in united spirit and purpose, striving side by side and contending with a single mind for the faith of the glad tidings (the Gospel). They are not for a moment frightened or intimidated in anything by their opponents and adversaries, for such [constancy and fearlessness] will be a clear sign (proof and seal) to their enemies of [their impending] destruction; but [a sure token and evidence] to the congregation of their deliverance and salvation, and that from You, God.

The membership of _____ fills up and completes my joy by living in harmony and being of the same mind and one in purpose, having the same love, being in full accord and of one harmonious mind and intention.

Scripture References (AMP)

Philippians 1:4-7a,8-11,25,26,27b,28
Philippians 2:2

38
PROTECTION FROM TERRORISM

Father, in the name of Jesus, we praise You and offer up thanksgiving because the Lord is near — He is coming soon. Therefore, we will not fret or have any anxiety about the terrorism that is threatening the lives of those who travel and those stationed on foreign soil or at home. But in this circumstance and in everything by prayer and petition [definite requests] with thanksgiving we continue to make our wants known to You.

Father, our petition is that terrorism in the heavenlies and on earth be stopped before it spreads to other countries and comes to our land, _____.

Jesus, You have given us the authority and power to trample upon serpents and scorpions, and (physical and mental strength and ability) over all the power that the enemy [possesses], and nothing shall in any way harm us.

Therefore, in the name of Jesus, we address and take authority over the prince of the power of the air and over the principalities, powers, the rulers of the darkness of this world, and spiritual wickedness in high places who have been assigned by Satan to terrorize God-fearing governments and their people.

Satan, we bind your works and render them null and void in the name of Jesus Christ of Nazareth, and we forbid you to operate in _____. We cast you out of our land and other God-fearing countries and command you to turn back in this day as we cry out; for this we know, that God is for us — and if God be for us who can be against us?

In the name of Jesus, we take authority over a spirit of timidity — of cowardice, of craven and cringing and fawning fear (of terrorism) — for [God has given us a spirit] of power and of love and of calm and well-balanced mind and discipline and self-control.

We shall not be afraid of the terror of the night, nor of the arrow [the evil plots and slanders of the wicked] that flies by day, nor of the pestilence that stalks in darkness, nor of the destruction and sudden death that surprise and lay waste at noonday.

Therefore, we establish ourselves on righteousness — right, in conformity with God's will and order; we shall be far even from the thought of oppression or destruction, for we shall not fear; and from terror, for it shall not come near us.

Holy Spirit, thank You for writing this Word upon the tablets of our hearts so that we can speak it out of our mouths, for we will order our conversation aright and You will show us the salvation of God. Hallelujah!

Scripture References

Philippians 4:5,6b AMP

Luke 10:19 AMP

Ephesians 6:10 AMP

Ephesians 2:2 AMP

Ephesians 6:12 AMP

Matthew 16:19

Psalm 56:9 AMP

Romans 8:31b AMP

2 Timothy 1:7 AMP

Psalm 91:5,6 AMP

Isaiah 54:14 AMP

Proverbs 3:3b AMP

Psalm 50:23

39

PROTECTION AND DELIVERANCE OF A CITY

Father, in the name of Jesus, we have received Your power — ability, efficiency, and might — because the Holy Spirit has come upon us; and we are Your witnesses in _____ and to the ends — the very bounds — of the earth.

We fearlessly and confidently and boldly draw near to the throne of grace that we may receive mercy and find grace to help in good time for every need — appropriate help and well-timed help, coming just when we in the city of _____ need it.

Father, thank You for sending forth Your commandments to the earth; Your Word runs very swiftly throughout _____. Your Word continues to grow and spread.

Father, we seek — inquire for, require and request — the peace and welfare of _____ in which You have caused us to live. We pray to You for the welfare of this city and do our part by getting involved in it. We will not let [false] prophets and diviners who are in our midst deceive us; we pay no attention and attach no significance to our dreams which we dream, or to

113

theirs. Destroy [their schemes], O Lord; confuse their tongues; for we have seen violence and strife in the city.

Holy Spirit, we ask You to visit our city and open the eyes of the people, that they may turn from darkness to light, and from the power of Satan to God, so that they may thus receive forgiveness and release from their sins and a place and portion among those who are consecrated and purified by faith in Jesus.

Father, we pray for deliverance and salvation for those who are following the course and fashion of this world — who are under the sway of the tendency of this present age — following the prince of the power of the air.

Father, forgive them, for they know not what they do.

We speak to the prince of the power of the air, to the god of this world who blinds the unbelievers' minds (that they should not discern the truth), and we command that he leave the heavens above our city.

Thank You, Father, for the guardian angels assigned to this place who war for us in the heavenlies.

In the name of Jesus, we stand victorious over the principalities, powers, rulers of the darkness of this world, and spiritual wickedness in high places over _____ .

Father, You said that morning after morning You will root up all the wicked in the land, that You may eliminate all the evildoers from the city of the Lord. We ask the Holy Spirit to sweep through the gates of our city and convince the people and bring demon-

stration to them about sin and about righteousness —
uprightness of heart and right standing with God —
and about judgment.

Father, You said, **For I know the thoughts and
plans that I have for you, . . . thoughts and plans for
welfare and peace, and not for evil, to give you hope
in your final outcome** (Jer. 29:11 AMP). By the blessing
of the influence of the upright and God's favor [because of
them] the city of _____ is exalted.

Scripture References

Acts 1:8 AMP	Luke 23:34a AMP
Hebrews 4:16 AMP	2 Corinthians 4:4 AMP
Psalm 147:15 AMP	Daniel 10:20,21 AMP
Acts 12:24 AMP	Ephesians 6:12
Jeremiah 29:7,8 AMP	Psalm 101:8 AMP
Psalm 55:9 AMP	John 16:8 AMP
Acts 26:18 AMP	Jeremiah 29:11 AMP
Ephesians 2:2 AMP	Proverbs 11:11a AMP

40

HEDGE OF PROTECTION

Father, in the name of Jesus, we lift up
_____ to You and pray a hedge of protection
around him/her. We thank You, Father, that You are
a wall of fire round about _____ and that you
set Your angels round about him/her.

We thank You, Father, that _____ dwells
in the secret place of the Most High and abides under
the shadow of the Almighty. We say of You, Lord, You
are his/her refuge and fortress, in You will he/she trust.
You cover _____ with Your feathers, and under
Your wings shall he/she trust. _____ shall not
be afraid of the terror by night or the fiery dart that flies
by day. Only with his/her eyes will _____ behold
and see the reward of the wicked.

Because _____ has made You, Lord,
his/her refuge and fortress, no evil shall befall him/her
— no accident will overtake him/her — neither shall any
plague or calamity come near him/her. For you give
Your angels charge over _____, to keep him/her
in all Your ways.

Father, because You have set your love upon
_____, therefore will You deliver him/her.
_____ shall call upon You, and You will answer

him/her. You will be with him/her in trouble, and will
satisfy _____ with long life and show him/her
Your salvation. Not a hair of his/her head shall perish.

Scripture References

Zechariah 2:5	Psalm 91:8-11
Psalm 34:7	Psalm 91:14-16
Psalm 91:1,2	Luke 21:18
Psalm 91:4,5	

41
PROSPERITY

Father, in the name of Jesus, I praise You with my whole heart. I praise You for Your mighty acts, and according to the abundance of Your greatness! Through faith in the name of Jesus, I say that _____ has received and enjoys life — and has it in abundance — to the full, till it overflows!

Father, according to Your Word, it is Your desire that _____ may prosper and be in health, even as his/her soul prospers. In the name of Jesus, I declare that _____ gets rid of all uncleanness and the rampant outgrowth of wickedness, and in a humble (gentle, modest) spirit receives and welcomes the Word which implanted and rooted [in his/her heart] contains the power to save his/her soul. In the name of Jesus, I affirm that he/she will diligently obey the message; being a doer of the Word, and not merely a listener to it.

I state that his/her delight and desire are in the law of the Lord, and on His law — the precepts, the instructions, the teachings of God — he/she habitually meditates (ponders and studies) by day and by night. Then he/she shall be like a tree firmly planted [and tended] by the streams of water, ready to bring forth his/her fruit in his/her season; his/her leaf also shall not fade or wither, and everything he/she does shall prosper [and come to maturity].

Holy Spirit, Jesus said that You will bring all things to his/her remembrance. Therefore, I decree that he/she will (earnestly) remember the Lord his/her God; for it is You Who gives _____ power to get wealth, that You may establish Your covenant which You swore to our fathers.

Father, I attest that out of the abundance of his/her heart _____ shall say continually, Let the Lord be magnified, Who takes pleasure in the prosperity of His servant. And his/her tongue shall talk of Your righteousness, rightness, and justice, and [his/her reason for] Your praise all the day long.

Scripture References

Psalm 9:1	Psalm 1:2,3 AMP
Psalm 150:2 AMP	John 14:26b
John 10:10b AMP	Deuteronomy 8:18 AMP
3 John 2	Matthew 12:34
James 1:21,22 AMP	Psalm 35:27b,28 AMP

42

DELIVERANCE FROM
MENTAL DISORDER

Father, in the name of Jesus, I fearlessly and
confidently and boldly draw near to the throne of grace;
that I may receive mercy and find grace to help in good
time for _____.

It is my prayer that _____ will come to the
knowledge of the truth and be saved from destruction.
Father, according to Psalm 107:20, You sent Your Word
and healed _____ and delivered him/her from
all his/her destructions. I am calling upon You in the
day of trouble, asking You to deliver _____,
and in the name of Jesus he/she shall honor and glorify
You. Father, I thank You for delivering his/her soul
from death, and his/her feet from falling, so that he/she
may walk before You in the light of the living.

It is You, Father, Who delivers _____ from
the pit and corruption of _____ (name of disorder:
schizophrenia, paranoia, manic depression, etc.) Father, You have not
given _____ a spirit of timidity — of cowardice,
of craven and cringing and fawning fear — but [You
have given him/her a spirit of] power and of love and

120

of calm and well-balanced mind and discipline and self-control.

In the name of Jesus, I forgive _____ his/her sins and stand in the gap for him/her until he/she comes to his/her senses [and] escapes out of the snare of the devil, who has held him/her captive.

Satan, I stand against you, your principalities, and powers, your rulers of the darkness of this world, and spiritual wickedness in high places which have been assigned to _____. *It is our God Who delivers* _____ *from the authority of darkness, and translates* _____ *into the Kingdom of His dear Son.*

I decree and declare that the law of the Spirit of Life in Christ Jesus has made _____ free from the law of sin and death. _____ shall no longer be of two minds — hesitating, dubious, irresolute — unstable and unreliable and uncertain about everything (he/she thinks, feels, and decides). _____ shall get rid of all uncleanness and the rampant outgrowth of wickedness, and in a humble (gentle, modest) spirit receive and welcome the Word which implanted and rooted [in his/her heart] contains the power to save his/her soul *(mind, will, and emotions).*

In the name of Jesus, grace be to _____ and peace from God our Father, and from the Lord Jesus Christ, Who gave Himself for his/her sin so that He might deliver him/her from this present evil world, according to the will of God, and our Father, to Whom be glory for ever and ever. Amen.

Prayers That Avail Much — Volume II

Scripture References

Hebrews 4:16 AMP

Psalm 50:15

Psalm 56:13

Psalm 103:4a AMP

2 Timothy 1:7 AMP

John 20:23 AMP

2 Timothy 2:26 AMP

Ephesians 6:12

Colossians 1:13

Romans 8:2

James 1:8,21 AMP

Galatians 1:3-5

122

43

OVERCOMING INFIDELITY

Father, I thank You that You hear my prayer, for I come in the name of Jesus and on the authority of Your Word. I come boldly to the throne of grace to receive mercy and find grace to help on behalf of _____ and _____. I take my place — standing in the gap — against the devil and his demons until the salvation of God is manifested in their lives. Father, I forgive them for their sins and stand firm knowing that the Holy Spirit will convict and convince them of sin, righteousness and judgment.

The wife, _____, is sane and sober-minded, temperate, and disciplined. She loves her husband and their children, and she confines herself to them. She is self-controlled, chaste, good-natured and kindhearted, adapting and subordinating herself to her husband, that the Word of God may not be exposed to reproach — blasphemed or discredited.

In a similar way, her husband, _____, is self-restrained and prudent, taking life seriously. He drinks waters out of his own cistern [of pure marriage relationship], and fresh running waters out of his own well — lest his offspring be dispersed abroad as water-brooks in the street. He confines himself to his own

123

wife, and their children will be for them alone and not the children of strangers with them. His fountain of human life is blessed with the rewards of fidelity, and he rejoices with the wife of his youth. He lets his wife be to him as the loving hind and pleasant doe [tender, gentle, attractive]. He lets her bosom satisfy him at all times; and he is transported with delight in her love.

The husband submits himself to Christ, Who is the head of the man. The husband is the head of his own wife, and they are subject one to the other out of reverence for Christ.

Thank You, Father, for hearing my prayer on behalf of this family. I know that You watch over Your Word to perform it, in Jesus' name.

Scripture References (AMP)

Titus 2:4-6   1 Corinthians 11:3
Proverbs 5:15-19   Ephesians 5:21
Hebrews 9:14   Jeremiah 1:12

44
OVERCOMING REJECTION
IN MARRIAGE

Father, in the name of Jesus, _____ and
_____ are delivered from this present evil age by the
Son of the Living God, and whom the Son has set free
is free indeed. Therefore, they are delivered from a spirit
of rejection and accepted in the Beloved to be holy and
blameless in His sight. They forgive all those who have
wronged them, and their hurts from the past are healed,
for Jesus came to heal the brokenhearted.

They are God's chosen people, holy and dearly
loved. They clothe themselves with compassion,
kindness, humility, gentleness, and patience. They bear
with each other and forgive whatever grievances they
may have against one another. They forgive as the Lord
forgave them. Over all these virtues, they put on love,
which binds them together in perfect unity.

When they were children, they talked like children,
thought like children, and reasoned like children, but
now they have become husband and wife, and they are
done with childish ways and have put them aside.

The blood of Christ, Who through the eternal Spirit
offered himself without spot to God, purges their

consciences from dead works of selfishness, agitating pasions, and moral conflicts, so they can serve the living God. They touch not any unclean thing, for they are a son and daughter of the most high God. Satan's power over them is broken and his strongholds are torn down. Sin no longer has dominion over them and their household.

The love of God reigns supreme in their home, and the peace of God acts as an umpire in all situations, Jesus is their Lord — spirit, soul, and body.

Scripture References (AMP)

Galatians 1:4	Romans 6:18
John 8:36	Colossians 3:12-15
Ephesians 1:16	1 Corinthians 13:11
Luke 4:18	1 Thessalonians 5:23

45

COMPLETE IN HIM AS A SINGLE

Father, we thank You that _____ desires and earnestly seeks first after the things of Your Kingdom. We thank You that he knows that You love him and that he can trust Your Word.

For in Jesus the whole fullness of Diety (the Godhead) continues to dwell in bodily form — giving complete expression of the Divine Nature, and _____ is in Him and has come to the fullness of life in Christ. He is filled with the Godhead — Father, Son, and Holy Spirit — and he reaches full spiritual stature. And Christ is the head of all rule and authority — of every angelic principality and power.

So because of Jesus, _____ is complete; Jesus is his/her Lord. He/she comes before You, Father, desiring a born again Christian mate. We petition that Your will be done in his/her life. Now we enter into that blessed rest by adhering, trusting in, and relying on You, in the name of Jesus.

Scripture References (AMP)

Colossians 2:9,10   Hebrews 4:10

127

46

OVERCOMING NEGATIVE
WORK ATTITUDES

Thank You, Father, for watching over Your Word to perform it. _____ is obedient to his/her employers — bosses or supervisors — having respect for them and eager to please them, in singleness of motive and with all his/her heart, as service to Christ. Not in the way of eyeservice — as if they were watching him/her — but as a servant (employee) of Christ, doing the will of God heartily and with his/her whole soul.

_____ readily renders service with goodwill, as to the Lord and not to men. He/she knows that for whatever good he/she does, he/she will receive his/her reward from the Lord.

_____ will do all things without grumbling, faultfinding, and complaining against God, and questioning and doubting within himself/herself. He/she is blameless and harmless, a child of God, without rebuke, in the midst of a crooked and perverse nation, among whom he/she shines as a light in the world.

He/she reveres the Lord, and his/her work is a sincere expression of his/her devotion to Him. Whatever may be his/her task, he/she works at it heartily from

the soul, as something done for God. The One Whom
_____ is actually serving is the Lord.

Scripture References (AMP)

Ephesians 6:5-8   Philippians 2:14,15
Colossians 3:22-24

47

COMFORT FOR A PERSON WHO HAS LOST A CHRISTIAN LOVED ONE

Father, I thank You that we have a High Priest Who is able to understand and sympathize and have a fellow feeling with _____'s weaknesses and infirmities (grief over the loss of his/her_____). Therefore, I fearlessly and confidently and boldly draw near to the throne of grace; that _____ may receive mercy and find grace to help in good time for every need — appropriate and well-timed help, coming just when _____ needs it.

Father, I thank You that _____ does not sorrow, as one who has no hope, because he/she believes that Jesus died and rose again; even so his/her loved one also who sleeps in Jesus will God bring back with Him. I ask that You comfort _____, for You said, **Blessed are they that mourn: for they shall be comforted** (Matt. 5:4).

Jesus, You have come to heal the brokenhearted. It is in the name of Jesus that You, Father, comfort _____ because You have loved him/her and

130

have given him/her everlasting consolation and good hope through grace.

Blessed be God, even the Father of our Lord Jesus Christ, the Father of mercies, and the God of all comfort; Who comforts _____ in all his/her tribulation, that he/she may be able to comfort those which are in any trouble, by the comfort wherewith he himself/she herself is comforted by God.

Father, thank You for appointing unto _____ who mourns in Zion, to give unto him/her beauty for ashes, the oil of joy for mourning, the garment of praise for the spirit of heaviness; that he/she might be called a tree of righteousness, the planting of the Lord, that You might be glorified.

Scripture References

Hebrews 4:15,16 AMP	2 Thessalonians 2:16
1 Thessalonians 4:13b,14	2 Corinthians 1:3,4
Matthew 5:4	Isaiah 61:3
Luke 4:18	

48
CHILDREN AT SCHOOL

Father, I confess Your Word this day concerning my children as they pursue their education and training at school. You are effectually at work in them creating within them the power and desire to please You. They are the head and not the tail, above and not beneath.

I pray that my children will find favor, good understanding and high esteem in the sight of God and their teachers and classmates. I ask You to give my children wisdom and understanding as knowledge is presented to them in all fields of study and endeavor.

Father, thank You for giving my children an appreciation for education and helping them to understand that the Source and beginning of all knowledge is You. They have the appetite of the diligent and they are abundantly supplied with educational resources, and their thoughts are those of the steadily diligent which tend only to achievement. Thank You that they are growing in wisdom and knowledge. I will not cease to pray for them, asking that they be filled with the knowledge of Your will bearing fruit in every good work.

Father, I thank You that my children have divine protection since they dwell in the secret place of the

Most High. My children trust and find their refuge in You and stand rooted and grounded in Your love. They shall not be led astray by philosophies of men and teaching that is contrary to Truth. You are their shield and buckler protecting them from attacks or threats. Thank You for the angels which You have assigned to them to accompany, defend and preserve them in all their ways of obedience and service. My children are established in Your love which drives all fear out of doors.

I pray that the teachers of my children will be godly men and women of integrity. Give our teachers understanding hearts and wisdom in order that they may walk in the ways of piety and virtue, revering Your Holy Name.

Scripture References

Philippians 2:13	Psalm 91:1,2
Deuteronomy 28:1,2,13	Ephesians 4:14
Proverbs 3:4	Psalm 91:3-11
1 Kings 4:29	Ephesians 1:17
Daniel 1:4	Psalm 112:8
Proverbs 1:4,7	Ephesians 3:17
Proverbs 3:13	Matthew 18:18
Proverbs 4:5	James 1:5
Colossians 1:9,10	

49
CHILD'S FUTURE

Father, Your Word declares that children are an inheritance from You and promises peace when they are taught in Your ways. I dedicate _____ to You today, that he/she might be raised as You would desire and will follow the path You would choose. Father, I confess Your Word this day over _____. I thank You that Your Word goes out and will not return unto You void, but will accomplish what it says it will do.

Heavenly Father, I commit myself, as a parent, to train _____ in the way he/she should go, trusting in the promise that he/she will not depart from Your ways, but will grow and prosper in them. I turn the care and burden of raising him/her over to You. I will not provoke my child, but will nurture and love him/her in Your care. I will do as the Word of God commands and teach my child diligently. My child will be upon my heart and mind. Your grace is sufficient to overcome my inabilities as a parent.

My child _____ is obedient and honors both his/her parents, being able to accept the abundant promises of Your Word of long life and prosperity. _____ is a godly child; not ashamed or afraid to honor and keep Your Word. He/She stands convinced that You are the Almighty God. I am thankful that as _____ grows, he/she will remember You and not pass by the opportunity of a relationship with Your Son, Jesus. Your great blessings will be upon _____ for keeping Your ways. I thank You for Your blessings over every area of _____'s life, that You will see to the salvation and obedience of his/her life to Your ways.

Heavenly Father, I thank You now that laborers will be sent into _____'s path, preparing the way for salvation, as it is written in Your Word, through Your Son, Jesus. I am thankful that _____ will recognize the traps of the devil and will be delivered to salvation through the purity of Your Son. You have given _____ the grace and the strength to walk the narrow pathway to Your kingdom.

I pray that just as Jesus increased in wisdom and stature, You would bless this child with the same wisdom and pour out Your favor and wisdom openly to him/her.

I praise You in advance for _____'s future spouse. Father, Your Word declares that you desire for children to be pure and honorable, waiting upon marriage. I speak blessings to the future union and believe that _____ will be well suited to his/her partner and their household will be in godly order, holding fast to the love of Jesus Christ. Continue to prepare _____ to be the man/woman of God that You desire him/her to be.

_____ shall be diligent and hard-working, never being lazy or undisciplined. Your Word promises great blessing to his/her house and he/she shall always be satisfied and will always increase. Godliness is profitable unto his/her house, and _____ shall receive the promise of life and all that is to come.

Father, thank You for protecting and guiding my child.

Scripture References

Psalm 127:3	Matthew 7:14
Isaiah 54:13	Luke 2:52
Isaiah 55:11	Hebrews 13:4
Proverbs 22:6	1 Thessalonians 4:3
1 Peter 5:7	Ephesians 5:22-25
Ephesians 6:4	2 Timothy 1:13
Deuteronomy 6:7	Proverbs 13:11
2 Corinthians 12:9	Proverbs 20:13
Ephesians 6:1-3	Romans 12:11
2 Timothy 1:12	1 Timothy 4:8
Proverbs 8:17,32	1 John 3:8
Luke 19:10	John 10:10
Matthew 9:38	Matthew 18:18
2 Corinthians 2:11	John 14:13
2 Timothy 2:26	Psalm 91:1,11
Job 22:30	

50

PRAYER FOR A
REBELLIOUS TEENAGER

Father, in the name of Jesus I affirm Your Word over my son/daughter who is in rebellion toward us, his/her parents. I cast the cares and the burden of this situation over on You, trusting You to sustain me and my child. I commit _____ to You and delight myself also in You, looking to the fulfillment of a solution. I know that where there is no way, Jesus is the Way. With thanksgiving I ask You to deliver _____ out of rebellion into right relationship with us, his/her parents.

Father, the first commandment with a promise is to the child who obeys his/her parents in the Lord. You said that all will be well with him/her and he/she will live long on the earth. I affirm this promise on behalf of my child asking You to give _____ an obedient spirit that he/she may honor (esteem and value as precious) his/her father and mother.

Father, forgive me for mistakes made out of my own unresolved hurts or selfishness which may have caused _____ hurt. I release the anointing that is upon Jesus to bind up and heal our (parents' and child's) broken hearts. Give us the ability to understand

and forgive one another as God for Christ's sake has forgiven us. Thank You for the Holy Spirit Who leads us into all truth and corrects erroneous perceptions about past or present situations.

Thank You for teaching us to listen to each other and giving _____ an ear that hears admonition for then he/she will be called wise. I affirm that I will speak excellent and princely things and the opening of my lips shall be for right things. Father, I commit to train and teach _____ in the way that he/she is to go and when _____ is old he/she will not depart from sound doctrine and teaching, but will follow it all the days of his/her life. In the name of Jesus, I command rebellion to be far from the heart of my child and confess that he/she is willing and obedient, free to enjoy the reward of Your promises. _____ shall be peaceful bringing peace to others.

Father, according to Your Word we have been given the ministry of reconciliation and I release this ministry and the word of reconciliation into this family situation. I refuse to provoke or irritate or fret my child, I will not be hard on him/her lest he/she becomes discouraged, feeling inferior and frustrated. I will not break his/her spirit in the Name of Jesus and by the power of the Holy Spirit. Father, I forgive my child for the wrongs which he/she has done and stand in the gap until he/she comes to his/her senses and escapes out of the snare of the enemy (rebellion). Thank You for watching over Your Word to perform it, turning and reconciling the heart of the rebellious child to the parents and the hearts of the parents to the child. Thank You for bringing my child back into a healthy relationship with You and with me that our lives might glorify You!

Scripture References

Psalm 55:12-14	Proverbs 8:6,7
1 Peter 5:7	Proverbs 22:6
Psalm 37:4	Isaiah 1:19
John 14:6	Isaiah 54:13
Ephesians 6:1-3	2 Corinthians 5:18,19
1 John 1:9	Colossians 3:21
Isaiah 61:1	John 20:23
John 16:13	Ezekiel 22:30
Proverbs 15:31	Jeremiah 1:12
Proverbs 13:1	Malachi 4:6

ANSWERED PRAYER REGISTER

And this is the confidence that we have in him, that, if we ask any thing according to his will, he heareth us:

And if we know that he hear us, whatsoever we ask, we know that we have the petitions that we desired of him.

1 John 5:14,15

Date	Explanation
_____	_____
_____	_____
_____	_____
_____	_____
_____	_____
_____	_____
_____	_____
_____	_____
_____	_____
_____	_____
_____	_____
_____	_____
_____	_____
_____	_____
_____	_____
_____	_____
_____	_____
_____	_____
_____	_____

ANSWERED PRAYER
REGISTER

And this is the confidence that we have in him, that, if we ask any thing according to his will, he heareth us:

And if we know that he hear us, whatsoever we ask, we know that we have the petitions that we desired of him.

1 John 5:14,15

Date	Explanation

ANSWERED PRAYER REGISTER

And this is the confidence that we have in him, that, if we ask any thing according to his will, he heareth us:

And if we know that he hear us, whatsoever we ask, we know that we have the petitions that we desired of him.

1 John 5:14,15

Date	Explanation

ANSWERED PRAYER REGISTER

And this is the confidence that we have in him, that, if we ask any thing according to his will, he heareth us:

And if we know that he hear us, whatsoever we ask, we know that we have the petitions that we desired of him.

1 John 5:14,15

Date	Explanation
_____	_____
_____	_____
_____	_____
_____	_____
_____	_____
_____	_____
_____	_____
_____	_____
_____	_____
_____	_____
_____	_____
_____	_____
_____	_____
_____	_____
_____	_____
_____	_____
_____	_____
_____	_____

SALVATION REGISTER

For God so loved the world, that he gave his only begotten Son, that whosoever believeth in him should not perish, but have everlasting life.

John 3:16

Spiritual Birthdate	Name
———	—————————
———	—————————
———	—————————
———	—————————
———	—————————
———	—————————
———	—————————
———	—————————
———	—————————
———	—————————
———	—————————
———	—————————
———	—————————
———	—————————
———	—————————
———	—————————
———	—————————
———	—————————
———	—————————
———	—————————
———	—————————
———	—————————
———	—————————

SALVATION REGISTER

For God so loved the world, that he gave his only begotten Son, that whosoever believeth in him should not perish, but have everlasting life.

John 3:16

Spiritual Birthdate   **Name**

HEALING REGISTER

Surely he hath borne our griefs, and carried our
sorrows: yet we did esteem him stricken, smitten of
God, and afflicted.

But he was wounded for our transgressions, he was
bruised for our iniquities: the chastisement of our
peace was upon him; and with his stripes we are
healed.

Isaiah 53:4,5

Healed of   **Date**

_____   _____

_____   _____

_____   _____

_____   _____

_____   _____

_____   _____

_____   _____

_____   _____

_____   _____

_____   _____

_____   _____

_____   _____

_____   _____

_____   _____

_____   _____

_____   _____

_____   _____

_____   _____

_____   _____

_____   _____

HEALING REGISTER

Surely he hath borne our griefs, and carried our sorrows: yet we did esteem him stricken, smitten of God, and afflicted.

But he was wounded for our transgressions, he was bruised for our iniquities: the chastisement of our peace was upon him; and with his stripes we are healed.

Isaiah 53:4,5

Healed of   **Date**

HEALING REGISTER

Surely he hath borne our griefs, and carried our sorrows: yet we did esteem him stricken, smitten of God, and afflicted.

But he was wounded for our transgressions, he was bruised for our iniquities: the chastisement of our peace was upon him; and with his stripes we are healed.

Isaiah 53:4,5

Healed of	Date

Pray with power!

The Prayers That Avail Much Family now has something for every member of your family! Designed specifically to help each person pray more effectively, each book is packed with scripture-based prayers or teaching on prayer. Pray with power — the power of God's Word!

A CALL TO PRAYER by Germaine Copeland, president of Word Ministries. Trade Paper. $7.99

PRAYERS THAT AVAIL MUCH, FOR FATHERS
A great gift idea for dad all year 'round. Black Bonded Leather. $19.95

PRAYERS THAT AVAIL MUCH, FOR MOTHERS
A gift for mom that shares your love any time of the year.
Dusty Rose Bonded Leather. $19.95

PRAYERS THAT AVAIL MUCH, FOR TEENS Written especially for teens! Mass Market Paper. $5.99

PRAYERS THAT AVAIL MUCH, SPECIAL EDITION The complete collection of volumes 1 & 2 — A great gift idea! Gray Bonded Leather. $19.95

PRAYERS THAT AVAIL MUCH FOR CHILDREN, BOOK 1 by Angela Brown. Full-color drawings and easy-to-read words teach children ages 2-8 the power of prayer. 11" x 8 1/2" Paper. $4.98

PRAYERS THAT AVAIL MUCH FOR CHILDREN, BOOK 2 from the Little Castle. More prayers for 2-8 year olds. 11" x 8 1/2" Paper. $4.98

AVAILABLE AT YOUR LOCAL CHRISTIAN BOOKSTORE.

Harrison House — on the cutting edge of Spirit-filled living.

Germaine Griffin Copeland is Founder and President of Word Ministries, Inc. As the daughter of a Church of God minister, she knew in her early teens that God was calling her into the ministry. Only after she was married and had four children did Germaine realize her desperate need to know God personally. As she reached out to Him, He moved in and "old things passed away, and behold all things became new."

In 1969 Germaine began to grow in the knowledge of God's love and in the reality of overcoming faith. In 1972 God opened doors for her to share what she had learned. She began teaching with Women's Aglow Fellowship and within a few years became a renowned conference speaker. Later, Word Ministries, Inc. was formed and in 1980 published *Prayers That Avail Much*. Since that time, Germaine has shared her love of God with truth and in simplicity to many in congregations and in many seminars throughout the country. In 1984 she was called to the office of pastor of Word of Life Christian Fellowship in Smyrna, Georgia.

Today Germaine balances her home and ministry with great wisdom and love. She ministers God's Word and the gifts of His Holy Spirit with tenderness and a deep desire to meet the needs of His people.

You may contact
Word Ministries
by writing:

Word Ministries, Inc.
38 Sloan St.
Roswell, GA 30075

Please include
your prayer requests
and comments when you write.

The Harrison House Vision

Proclaiming the truth and the power
of the Gospel of Jesus Christ
with excellence;

Challenging Christians to
live victoriously,
grow spiritually,
know God intimately.